M000073874

Presented to

_____

By

_____

Date

_____

flourish

DEVOTIONS FOR A WELL-TENDED HEART

MIKE BEAUMONT & MARTIN MANSER

Tyndale House Publishers, Inc.
Carol Stream, Illinois

LIVING EXPRESSIONS

COLLECTION

Living Expressions invites you to explore
God's Word in a way that is refreshing to
the spirit and restorative to the soul.

Visit Tyndale online at www.tyndale.com.

TYNDALE, Tyndale's quill logo, *Living Expressions*, and the Living Expressions logo
are registered trademarks of Tyndale House Publishers, Inc.

Flourish: Prayers for a Well-Tended Heart

Copyright © 2020 by Mike Beaumont and Martin Manser; all rights reserved.
Adapted and curated from *Walking with God: 365 Promises and Prayers from the Bible
for Every Day of the Year*, by Martin Manser and Mike Beaumont, copyright © 2005
by Eagle Publishing.

Designed by Jennifer Ghionzoli

Unless otherwise indicated, all Scripture quotations are taken from the *Holy Bible*,
New Living Translation, copyright © 1996, 2004, 2015 by Tyndale House
Foundation. Used by permission of Tyndale House Publishers, Inc., Carol Stream,
Illinois 60188. All rights reserved. Scripture quotations marked KJV are taken from
the *Holy Bible*, King James Version.

For information about special discounts for bulk purchases, please contact Tyndale
House Publishers at csresponse@tyndale.com, or call 1-800-323-9400.

ISBN 978-1-4964-4126-3

Printed in China

26   25   24   23   22   21   20
7   6   5   4   3   2   1

Look, the winter is past, and the rains are over and gone.
The flowers are springing up, the season of singing birds has come,
and the cooing of turtledoves fills the air.

SONG OF SONGS 2:11-12

Contents

Praying Right 2

A Sacrifice of Praise 4

Our Awesome God 6

Longing for More 8

Come Clean, Get Clean 10

Are My Prayers Selfish, Lord? 12

Counting the Cost 14

Don't Take Things for Granted 16

Praying for Others 18

The Power of Blessing 20

Get Wisdom! 22

Revival! 24

The Priority of Life 26

The God Who Comes to Help 28

A Question of Trust 30

Praying with Closed Eyes 32

Praying in Jesus' Name 34

Prayer Changes Things 36

Patience 38

Learning through Failure 40

An Undivided Heart 42

Teach Us to Pray 44

Our Father in Heaven 46

Keeping God's Name Holy 48

The Coming of God's Kingdom 50

Doing God's Will 52

Prayer for Present Needs 54

Prayer for Past Sin 56

Prayer for Future Welfare 58

The Whisper of His Power 60

Big Heart, Big Vision 62

Always There 64

An Encounter with Holiness 66

Put Your Belt On 68

Externals and Internals 70

Faith Is Not a Commodity 72

At the Breaking Point 74

Saying I'm Sorry 76

What's In It for Me? 78

Blame Shifting 80

Thirsty for God 82

Unanswered Prayer 84

The God of Flesh and Blood 86

When You Need a Breakthrough 88

When You're Down 90

Me, Me, Me 92

When God Feels Far Away 94

Praying in the Spirit 96

Just Stand! 98

The Lord, My Lover.....................................100

Complain to God!......................................102

Taking Time to Look 104

The Gift of Work 106

The Destructive Power of Jealousy 108

Worship That Releases Power...................110

In Anxious Times.......................................112

He Never Gives Up....................................114

Praying for My Nation...............................116

He's Praying for Me 118

No Retirement! 120

The God Who Leads...................................122

God, Our Redeemer 124

God Can Take Your Honesty......................126

The Joy of the Lord...................................128

Go-Getters for God 130

No Longer Slaves......................................132

The Family Likeness 134

God's Goodness and Ours........................136

When Trouble Comes 138

The Call to Kindness.................................140

Listening Changes Things 142

My Daddy!..144

The Blessing of True Friends.....................146

Waiting for the Whispers 148

Pressing On..150

Praying Right

Pour out your hearts like water to the Lord. LAMENTATIONS 2:19

Lord, I WANT TO GROW IN MY PRAYING, and I want to get it "right." But the minute I say those words, I have to stop. The thing is, my whole life is governed by trying to get things "right." I try to run my home "right," do my work "right," serve at church "right." And often I focus so much on doing things "right" that I lose my joy. The same is true with my praying sometimes: I get so caught up in thinking I need the "right" words that I lose the heart of it—just talking to you.

So today, Lord, I declare that prayer is first and foremost about my *relationship* with you; and as such, it has many different expressions. No one way is "right." I'm going to stop fussing and just start sharing my heart. I may not find the "right" words sometimes, but it doesn't matter. As long as my heart is in it, I know you love to hear me.

I remember the parable of the Pharisee and the tax collector praying in the Temple. The Pharisee looked and sounded fine; but he was talking to himself rather than to you—parading his own righteousness rather than seeking yours. The tax collector just prayed, "O God, be merciful to me, for I am a sinner." And you told us, Jesus, that it was he who went home justified.[1]

So I thank you that you aren't interested in the beauty of my language—just in what I share from my heart. *Amen.*

---

[1] Luke 18:9-14

God opposes the proud but
gives grace to the humble.

JAMES 4:6

PURPLE ECHINACEA

Purple echinacea are also
known as purple coneflowers
since their daisy-like petals
angle away from the brown
center, forming a cone.

A SACRIFICE
of Praise

Let us offer through Jesus a continual sacrifice of praise to God, proclaiming our allegiance to his name. HEBREWS 13:15

Lord, I KNOW I OUGHT TO PRAISE YOU IN EVERY SITUATION; but the truth is, I don't always find this easy. When life is tough or things aren't going well, praising you demands a real sacrifice—a sacrifice of my feelings, questions, and doubts.

But then I recall that whenever people in the Bible made this sacrifice, they always found you did not disappoint them, and blessing was always the final outcome. I think of Moses, David, Job, Jehoshaphat, Hannah, Zechariah and Elizabeth, Paul—and Jesus! All faced incredibly challenging circumstances, yet all sacrificed their feelings and put their trust in you. And you vindicated them.

Why could they do this, Lord? Because they knew you are the sovereign Lord. Even when things seem to be going wrong, you are still on your throne, still causing "everything to work together for the good of those who love God."[1] When I despair or moan, I'm really saying I don't believe that or I don't think you know what you're doing. But when I offer a sacrifice of praise, I'm declaring, "I may not understand you, but I commit myself to trusting you as I wait for your outcome!" Praise gets the focus off me and my situation and back on to you, who alone can redeem all things.

I may not always be able to rejoice in the *circumstances*, Lord; but I can always rejoice in *you*. So I set my heart today on bringing you a sacrifice of praise. *Amen.*

---

[1] Romans 8:28

I will praise the LORD at all times.

I will constantly speak his praises.

PSALM 34:1

BLOODROOT

Bloodroot, whose cheery flowers have distinct white petals and yellow stamens, has been used in cancer treatments and for inflammation, infections, and coughs.

OUR
Awesome God

Come, everyone! Clap your hands! Shout to God with joyful praise!
For the LORD Most High is awesome. He is the great King
of all the earth. PSALM 47:1-2

Lord, **THE PSALMIST WAS RIGHT:** You are awesome! Amazing! Breathtaking! Stunning! Magnificent! When I think of you and all that you have done, everything within me cries out, "Wow!"

So I joyfully respond to the invitation to "come." I clap my hands and shout joyful praise to you, because you, Lord, are worth getting excited about! The soccer fan might shout, the theatergoer might applaud, and the nature lover might sigh; but as one who knows you, I have far more cause for excitement than any of them. For as I come, I remember once again who you are and what you have done—especially all that you have done for me!

As I remember, I stand amazed at how truly awesome you are. The beauty and intricacies of your creation, your grace freely given to sinners, your faithfulness to your people in the past, your faithfulness to me, and your many acts of kindness—all these cause me to join with the psalmist and those who say, "Wow! What an awesome God!"

And there is even more. Your awesomeness also inspires awe in me—a deep sense of profound respect. For you are almighty God: a God who is holy, majestic, highly exalted, and far above all things. And yet you tell me not to stay at a distance, which is what I deserve, but to come. And that, Lord, is truly awesome. *Amen.*

Who is like you among the gods, O Lᴏʀᴅ—glorious in holiness, awesome in splendor, performing great wonders?

EXODUS 15:11

WINTER HELIOTROPE

Winter heliotrope's vanilla-scented flowers bloom in damp meadows and woodlands as well as along riverbanks. Its native range is southwestern and southeastern Europe and northern Africa.

LONGING
for More

The LORD replied to Moses, "I will indeed do what you have asked, for I look favorably on you, and I know you by name." Moses responded, "Then show me your glorious presence." EXODUS 33:17-18

Lord, I'M CHALLENGED BY MOSES' PRAYER. He knew you, and you knew him. And yet he wanted more—not more blessings from you, but simply more of yourself. I'm challenged by that since I often find myself coming to you for what I can get out of you. I live in a culture that always wants more, yet it's always more stuff, more blessing, more prosperity—things that put *us* at the center rather than you.

So I'm stirred by how Moses just wanted you. He could have asked for anything when he was up on Mount Sinai, but what he wanted more than anything else was simply more of your presence as he led your people. He even said, "If you don't personally go with us, don't make us leave this place."[1] And then I think of David, who said, "My soul thirsts for you; my whole body longs for you in this parched and weary land where there is no water."[2]

Such longing for you! And it challenges my heart. Am I as passionate to know more of you, or am I lukewarm and half-hearted at times? Today, Lord, I'm asking you to make me thirsty for more of you—and then to quench that thirst with your presence. For only when I am full of you can I overflow to others. *Amen.*

---

[1] Exodus 33:15 [2] Psalm 63:1

I want to know Christ
and experience the mighty power
that raised him from the dead.

PHILIPPIANS 3:10

BLUE BELLFLOWER
Blue bellflowers are part of a
diverse plant group, all with bell-
shaped blooms. These sun-loving,
brightly colored plants enjoy
cool and moderate
climates.

COME CLEAN,
Get Clean

People who conceal their sins will not prosper, but if they confess and turn from them, they will receive mercy. PROVERBS 28:13

Lord, I DON'T LIKE THE CONCEPT OF SIN. The very word reminds me there are standards, and that I don't always live up to them. It reminds me I'm not as good as I'd like to think I am. And you don't like the idea of sin either—though for very different reasons. I don't like it because it reminds me of my failings; and you don't like it because it offends your perfection. Your Word tells me you hate sin; that its foul stench gets up your nose and makes you turn away.[1]

Yet it also tells me you love to deal with sin! And through Christ, you have made provision for doing just that. But it all starts with me: recognizing sin for what it is; owning up to it; coming clean in order to get clean. I recall the promise in the Bible that "if we claim we have no sin, we are only fooling ourselves and not living in the truth. But if we confess our sins to him, he is faithful and just to forgive us our sins and to cleanse us from all wickedness."[2]

And so today, Lord, I choose not to run from my sin. Nor will I try to hide it. Rather, I choose to come clean in order to get clean. And as I do, I trust your promise that you will forgive me. *Amen.*

---

[1] Isaiah 65:1-5 [2] 1 John 1:8-9

Repent of your sins
and turn to God, so that your
sins may be wiped away.

ACTS 3:19

WILD LILAC

Wild lilac comes in many
varieties, from ground cover
types to bushes fifteen to twenty
feet tall. Overwatering and
overfeeding will weaken
this plant.

ARE MY PRAYERS
Selfish, Lord?

Don't worry about anything; instead, pray about everything. Tell God what you need, and thank him for all he has done. PHILIPPIANS 4:6

Lord, HERE I AM, asking for things for myself again. I sometimes think you must get tired of my coming to you with all my requests, and I wonder if maybe I'm just being selfish.

Yet I remember that your Word says I should never be embarrassed about bringing my personal needs to you. You are my heavenly Father who delights to hear the heart cries of your children, and you have committed yourself to answering them out of your rich resources. I'm encouraged to remember that Jesus himself urged us in the Lord's Prayer[1] to bring all our needs before you—prayers about our present circumstances, our past sins, and our future welfare.

In fact, as I think about it, I'm overwhelmed by the sheer breadth of personal needs that people in the Bible brought to you in prayer: daily provision, healing, marriage, children, protection, guidance, understanding, wisdom, forgiveness, strength, boldness, victory, rescue . . . All this reminds me that when we are secure in our relationship with you, there is absolutely nothing in life that we cannot bring to you.

So Lord, I want to "come boldly to the throne of our gracious God"[2] and bring bold and big requests to you today. And just like in the parable of the friend who needed bread[3] and the parable of the widow and the judge,[4] I resolve to keep asking until I have received what I need from you, my loving heavenly Father. *Amen.*

---

[1] Matthew 6:9-13 [2] Hebrews 4:16 [3] Luke 11:5-10 [4] Luke 18:1-7

You don't have what you want because you don't ask God for it.

JAMES 4:2

CALLIANDRA

Calliandra is a genus of tropical plants, evergreens, flowering shrubs, and trees. Its colorful blossoms resemble powder puffs.

COUNTING

the Cost

If any of you wants to be my follower, you must give up your own way,
take up your cross daily, and follow me. If you try to hang on
to your life, you will lose it. But if you give up your life
for my sake, you will save it. LUKE 9:23-24

Lord, I OFTEN FIND MYSELF counting the cost of things: adding up prices in stores, figuring out if I can afford that new car, judging whether a request for help will take up too much time. Counting the cost is a way of life for me—except when it comes to you.

Oh, I know there is no cost for *knowing* you—Jesus himself paid that through his death on the cross, and there's nothing I can add. But it's the cost of *following* you that I often balk at: the cost of living life your way, of being a disciple.

I'm challenged by the way you call me to change established loyalties. Everything I've put first in my life—family, work, friends, money, plans, future—you now call me to put second. Sometimes I find that hard, yet you say that what I cling to I will ultimately lose.

I know from experience that whenever I do put you first, I never lose out. So today, help me not only to count the cost but also to be ready to pay it. For I know that as I do, it will never be my loss. *Amen.*

Everyone who has given up houses or brothers or sisters or father or mother or children or property, for my sake, will receive a hundred times as much in return and will inherit eternal life.

MATTHEW 19:29

YARROW

Yarrow's tightly packed flowers attract butterflies and make excellent cut or dried arrangements. The plant is an herb that is often used medicinally.

for Granted

We prayed that he would give us a safe journey and protect us,
our children, and our goods as we traveled. . . . So we fasted
and earnestly prayed that our God would take care
of us, and he heard our prayer.   EZRA 8:21, 23

Lord, **I READ TODAY'S SCRIPTURE** and realize how I've slipped into taking the ordinary things of life for granted. I get in the car or jump on a plane without giving it a second thought. I just assume I'll be safe. And it's only when I read of some accident that I realize how fortunate I've been.

I know I don't need to live fearfully; yet Ezra's prayer is a provocation. For it wasn't just because the journey back to Jerusalem was full of dangers and difficulties, but because he wanted *you*, Lord, to be at the center of everything he did. He wanted the people to know that safety and protection weren't things to be taken for granted, but rather your precious gifts.

Of course, I could dismiss that kind of prayer as just more necessary in those days. But maybe the safety and comfort to which I've become accustomed has simply made me more casual, ungrateful, and presumptuous in deciding what to pray about.

Life today is still full of potential dangers, whether from things or people. So, Lord, help me to commit myself to you each day for your protection, without fear or panic and in an attitude of dependent trust. *Amen.*

Pray, too, that we will be rescued from wicked and evil people, for not everyone is a believer. But the Lord is faithful; he will strengthen you and guard you from the evil one.

2 THESSALONIANS 3:2-3

MUSCARI

Muscari is perhaps better known as grape hyacinth. Its cobalt-blue flowers cluster together and emit grape-juice scent.

PRAYING

for Others

The Holy Spirit helps us in our weakness. For example, we don't know what God wants us to pray for. But the Holy Spirit prays for us with groanings that cannot be expressed in words. ROMANS 8:26

Lord, THE MOST IMPORTANT THING IN LIFE is me—at least, that's what the world around me says. I'm constantly told to put myself first, to indulge myself, to think of "me." Even some Christians say the whole purpose of my relationship with you is for blessing me.

But it seems that's not what your Word tells me, Lord. It challenges me not to seek blessings for myself, but to seek blessings for others. And one way you call me to do that is through praying for them. I confess I find prayer a mystery; yet in the Bible I see that praying for others is a key means you have chosen for pouring out your blessings.

Sometimes I don't know how to pray for them, so thank you for your promise that if I will stop and listen, your Holy Spirit will lead me in my praying by dropping his thoughts into mine; and as I pray those thoughts, I will see your will in heaven put into action here on earth.

So what do I pray for my family and friends today? Blessing,[1] health,[2] protection,[3] spiritual growth[4]—Lord, all this and more besides! And for myself, increase my experience of Spirit-prompted praying, just as you have promised. *Amen.*

---

[1] 2 Chronicles 30:27 [2] 3 John 1:2 [3] Acts 12:5 [4] Colossians 4:12

I will pour out a spirit of grace and prayer on the family of David and on the people of Jerusalem.

ZECHARIAH 12:10

PRIMROSE

The primrose is a classic English woodland flower. It prefers shade over intense sun and needs consistent watering and good drainage.

THE POWER OF

Blessing

May the LORD bless you and protect you. May the LORD smile on you and be gracious to you. May the LORD show you his favor and give you his peace. NUMBERS 6:24-26

Lord, I LIVE IN A WORLD where we often say, "Bless you!" But sometimes it's just another way of saying "Thank you!" or "I hope things go well!" or even "Goodbye!" And sometimes it's just something we say because someone has sneezed.

But in your Word, blessing someone was far more serious and powerful than any of that. It was a powerful prayer of declaration based on your very own promises. That's why you commanded the priests to say this special blessing over your people. It was a purposeful statement of what you yourself wanted to do for them. And so in repeating it, the priests were saying, "Let it happen, Lord!"

Yes, let it happen, Lord! That's what I want to pray for others today. I want to bless my family and my friends, saying, "Let what you have promised happen for them, Lord!"

But now I've suddenly realized I shouldn't just bless my family and friends, but my enemies, too. For you said, "Bless those who curse you. Pray for those who hurt you."[1] And I find that harder, Lord.

So today, please help me to speak words of blessing over everyone—even my enemies and those who hinder or oppose me. And then help me to do all I can to bring that blessing about. *Amen.*

---

[1] Luke 6:28

Jesus . . . took the children in his arms and placed his hands on their heads and blessed them.

MARK 10:14-16

BLACK-EYED SUSAN

Black-eyed Susans are part of the sunflower family. They appear as sunny spots of joy in gardens and meadows throughout their native North America.

Get Wisdom!

Don't turn your back on wisdom, for she will protect you.
Love her, and she will guard you. Getting wisdom is the wisest thing
you can do! And whatever else you do, develop good judgment.
If you prize wisdom, she will make you great. Embrace her,
and she will honor you. PROVERBS 4:6-8

Lord, I DON'T OFTEN PRAY FOR WISDOM—except when a crisis occurs. Yet prayers for wisdom—the ability to do the *right thing* in the *right way* at the *right time*—are scattered throughout your Word.

I think of King Solomon. You told him to ask for whatever he wanted, and instead of asking for wealth or power, he prayed, "Give me an understanding heart so that I can govern your people well and know the difference between right and wrong."[1]

And you replied, "Because you have asked for wisdom in governing my people with justice and have not asked for a long life or wealth or the death of your enemies—I will give you what you asked for! I will give you a wise and understanding heart such as no one else has had or ever will have! And I will also give you what you did not ask for—riches and fame!"[2] In asking for wisdom, Solomon received not only that, but much more besides.

So today, Lord, I pray for your Spirit's gift of wisdom.[3] May I be like Jesus, who "grew in wisdom and in stature and in favor with God and all the people."[4] Increase my wisdom, that I may both be blessed and be a blessing. *Amen*.

---

[1] Kings 3:9 [2] 1 Kings 3:11-13 [3] 1 Corinthians 12:8 [4] Luke 2:52

If you need wisdom, ask our generous God, and he will give it to you.

He will not rebuke you for asking.

JAMES 1:5

SIBERIAN WALLFLOWER
Fragrant and vibrant yellow-orange Siberian wallflowers typically bloom in their second year. They return as bright spots of sunshine year after year.

Revival!

Won't you revive us again, so your people
can rejoice in you? PSALM 85:6

Lord, THE WORD *REVIVAL* EXCITES MY HEART! When I read of historic revivals or hear about revivals around the world today, my heart is stirred with a longing that cries out for you to bring revival to my own country; to make the church even more alive so that prodigals come home, sinners are saved, and the nation is changed.

I remember your promise to Solomon when he dedicated the Temple in Jerusalem: "If my people who are called by my name will humble themselves and pray and seek my face and turn from their wicked ways, I will hear from heaven and will forgive their sins and restore their land."[1] Your words remind me that revival begins not with sinners, but with saints—with your own people.

I acknowledge that it is as we see our own desperate need for you that your Spirit begins to move, first in us and then in those around us. Therefore, help me to humble myself and walk before you with a repentant heart. May I not be like those to whom Jesus had to say, "You don't love me or each other as you did at first!"[2] and "You have a reputation for being alive—but you are dead."[3]

Lord, help me today to listen to your Spirit and to do what he says. And as I do, may revival begin with me. *Amen.*

---

[1] 2 Chronicles 7:14 [2] Revelation 2:4 [3] Revelation 3:1

I have heard all about you, LORD. I am filled with awe by your amazing works. In this time of our deep need, help us again as you did in years gone by.

HABAKKUK 3:2

SEA FIG
The magenta-flowered sea fig succulent originated in South Africa and today is found in South America and along the California and Oregon coasts.

THE PRIORITY

of Life

Seek the Kingdom of God above all else, and live righteously,
and he will give you everything you need. MATTHEW 6:33

Lord, I SEEM TO HAVE SO MANY PRIORITIES in life that consume my time and energy. But today's Scripture reminds me that as a follower of Jesus, I really have only one priority: to seek first the Kingdom of God.

Right away I can think of so many reasons why this just isn't . . . practical. After all, there's money to be earned, a family to look after, and a home to be kept. Yet Jesus issued his challenge after telling his disciples not to worry about such basic necessities of life as food and clothing—the very things that *are* my priorities so often. He said that if we get this new priority in place, then all these other concerns will work out okay.

I know he wasn't saying, "Just sit back and pray and all this stuff will drop out of heaven." Rather, he was challenging what we prioritize, what we focus on, what we pursue. He was saying, "Don't seek what *you* want first; seek what *God* wants first." And that sounds hard—if not scary! But thank you that his words come with a promise: If we seek your Kingdom first, then all the practical necessities of life will start to fall into place.

So Lord, help me to hear Jesus' challenge today and take practical steps to respond to it. And thank you that as I do, you will be there to meet me and bless me. *Amen.*

Wherever your treasure is, there the desires of your heart will also be.

LUKE 12:34

DRUMMOND PHLOX

Drummond phlox, named after Scottish botanist Thomas Drummond, is a fragrant, red-bloomed annual. This Texas native grows throughout the southeastern United States.

THE GOD WHO
Comes to Help

I have certainly seen the oppression of my people in Egypt.
I have heard their cries of distress because of their harsh slave
drivers. Yes, I am aware of their suffering. So I have come down
to rescue them.   EXODUS 3:7-8

Lord, **WHAT AN AMAZING GOD YOU ARE!** Every other religion in the world has people reaching up to find their god; yet you are the God who comes down to find people and to help them!

I think of when the Israelites were slaves in Egypt, and you saw their suffering and heard their cries. You were concerned for their welfare and said, "I have come down to rescue them." And that simple sentence sums up how you have acted again and again for your people, for your very nature is always to be a redeeming God.

I think of how when Jesus came into this world, the same message characterized his life. At the start of his ministry, he read this passage from Isaiah in the synagogue at Nazareth: "The Spirit of the LORD is upon me, for he has anointed me to bring Good News to the poor. He has sent me to proclaim that captives will be released, that the blind will see, that the oppressed will be set free, and that the time of the LORD's favor has come."[1]

The time of your favor had come! And the time of your favor is still with us. So I thank you that you aren't a God who stands far off, but a God who comes to help his people—who comes to help me today. *Amen.*

---

[1] Luke 4:18-19

28

Praise the Lord, the God of Israel, because he has visited and redeemed his people.

LUKE 1:68

GREEN AGAVE

The green agave succulent has large leaves that form a rosette. The plant makes a striking focal point in a garden.

A QUESTION
of Trust

I am trusting you, O LORD, saying, "You are my God!"
My future is in your hands.   PSALM 31:14-15

Lord, I DON'T LIKE HARD TIMES. Yet no one gets through life without trouble or sorrow at one point or another. As Job's friend said, "People are born for trouble as readily as sparks fly up from a fire."[1] And when trouble comes my way, Lord, the first thing I do is ask, *Why?*

But I'm grateful I'm not alone in that; for many people in the Bible—the psalmists, Gideon, Jeremiah, Habakkuk[2]—asked you the same question. Even your Son asked *Why?* when he was suffering on the cross![3] And yet since their questions are recorded in your Word, I'm encouraged that you really don't mind when I bring my questions to you, even—especially—the hard ones.

But I know this doesn't necessarily mean I'll get an answer. For ultimately, the answer to *Why?* remains a mystery. And asking also doesn't get us very far. In fact, those who asked in the Bible rarely got an *answer*. What they got instead was an *encounter*—an encounter with you, the living God, who brings strength and encouragement in the midst of our troubles so we can walk through them and come out on the other side.

So Lord, instead of pouring my emotional and spiritual energy into a question that ultimately has no answer, at least this side of heaven, I'm choosing to do what those people in the Bible did—trust you—and as I do, to see again that you cause "everything to work together for the good of those who love [you]."[4]   *Amen.*

---

[1] Job 5:7   [2] Psalm 10:1; Psalm 42:9; Judges 6:13-14; Jeremiah 15:18; Habakkuk 1:3   [3] Matthew 27:46   [4] Romans 8:28

The eternal God is your refuge,
and his everlasting arms are under you.

DEUTERONOMY 33:27

BEACH MORNING GLORY

Beach morning glory is native to coastal North America. Its lengthy, tangled vines and deep roots make it a stabilizing cover for sand dunes.

Closed Eyes

"Don't be afraid!" Elisha told him. "For there are more on our side than on theirs!" Then Elisha prayed, "O LORD, open his eyes and let him see!" 2 KINGS 6:16-17

Lord, I OFTEN PRAY WITH MY EYES CLOSED. I don't mean my physical eyes, because I'm sure it doesn't matter whether they're closed or open. I mean my spiritual eyes, for I'm sure I often just don't "see" what I ought to.

That's why I'm struck by the story of Elisha's servant. For some time Israel had been doing well in their conflict against the Arameans, thanks to Elisha's prophetic insights that gave Israel "inside information." But finally, the king of Aram had had enough of Elisha and sent his army to capture him. When Elisha's servant woke up to find the town surrounded by troops, he ran to tell Elisha the bad news.

Yet Elisha, calm as anything, simply said, "There are more on our side than on theirs!" I'm sure the servant thought he'd gone crazy. But Elisha prayed that the servant's eyes would be opened—and suddenly "he saw that the hillside around Elisha was filled with horses and chariots of fire."[1] The enemy was completely outnumbered! Little wonder Elisha wasn't panicking.

So even today, Lord, please give me eyes that can *see*; eyes that can see the spiritual battle going on around me that I can't see with human eyes. *Amen.*

---

[1] 2 Kings 6:17

We are not fighting against flesh-and-blood enemies, but against evil rulers and authorities of the unseen world, against mighty powers in this dark world, and against evil spirits in the heavenly places. EPHESIANS 6:12

VIRGINIA ROSE
The Virginia rose offers year-round color: Dark-green foliage turns fiery in autumn, and pink flowers bloom in summer. Its red berries also make tasty jam!

in Jesus' Name

> *You can ask for anything in my name, and I will do it, so that the Son can bring glory to the Father. Yes, ask me for anything in my name, and I will do it!* JOHN 14:13-14

Lord, JESUS PROMISED to give me whatever I ask for in his name. Well, where should I begin? The kitchen needs remodeling, the car's getting older, and a raise at work would be nice . . .

But did you really mean that I just need to tell you what I want, and I'll get it? That's what Sceva's sons thought when they imitated exorcists who were praying for people in Jesus' name, and a man with an evil spirit replied, "I know Jesus, and I know Paul, but who are you?"[1] Then he beat them up! They certainly learned that praying "in Jesus' name" wasn't just a formula to get whatever they wanted.

Isn't praying "in Jesus' name" about praying on the basis of *who Jesus is* and *what Jesus has done*—your Son crucified to pay the penalty for my sins so that I might come boldly into your presence?

And isn't it about praying on the basis of *what Jesus is like*? For the "anything" that he promised must first agree with the "everything" that he is. He is holy, so how can I make an unholy request? He is selfless, so how can I ask for something that is selfish?

And it's also about praying on the basis of *what Jesus wants*— the continuing of his work on earth, not the meeting of my every need. Thank you that when I pray like this, you will surely hear and answer. *Amen.*

---

[1] Acts 19:15

I tell you the truth, you will ask the Father directly, and

he will grant your request

because you use my name.

JOHN 16:23

MAXIMILIAN SUNFLOWER

The Maximilian sunflower was named for Prince Maximilian of Wied-Neuwied, Germany, who explored the American West in the 1830s. It's also called the Michaelmas daisy.

Changes Things

He answered their prayer because
they trusted in him. 1 CHRONICLES 5:20

Lord, PEOPLE SOMETIMES ASK ME if prayer makes a difference, or how I know that what I prayed for wasn't just a coincidence.
All I know, Lord, is that a remarkable number of coincidences seem
to happen when I pray. With all my heart, I believe you hear and
answer my prayers, and that those answers change things and
people—including me.

And I'm encouraged to keep praying, because the Bible is full
of examples where things changed when people prayed: people
like Moses, who saw you rescue Israel from the Egyptians as he
raised his staff and called out to you; Hannah, whose childless-
ness ended through her faithful, persistent prayers; Elijah, who
witnessed countless miracles as he prayed you would demonstrate
your power in the face of the godless.

And there's also Hezekiah, whose life span was extended
because he prayed; Nehemiah, who saw amazing doors of
opportunity opened because he prayed; Daniel, who influenced
a whole nation because he prayed; Peter, who was miraculously
freed from jail because others prayed; and Paul, who experienced
prayer rescuing him from danger again and again.

Prayer truly changed things—in many contexts and for many
people. And Lord, I believe the same can still happen today, even
through my own prayers. So help me to keep faithfully bringing
them to you. *Amen.*

Elijah was as human as we are, and yet when he prayed earnestly that no rain would fall, none fell for three and a half years! Then, when he prayed again, the sky sent down rain and the earth began to yield its crops.

JAMES 5:17-18

STAR OF BETHLEHEM

Star of Bethlehem's white, star-shaped flowers shine among other spring blooms. They're best suited for contained areas since they tend to crowd other plants.

Patience

I waited patiently for the LORD to help me,
and he turned to me and heard my cry. PSALM 40:1

Lord, **PATIENCE ISN'T SOMETHING** that comes easily to me. When I'm stuck in traffic, or the children aren't cooperating, or the printer jams again, or I'm dealing with someone who's being difficult, it's all too easy to get impatient. And I know that getting impatient invariably leads to other sins too. But since the culture around me is one of impatience, with everyone wanting everything *now*, it isn't easy to change.

Yet your Word tells me that your Spirit wants to grow the fruit of patience in me.[1] And if patience is something that grows, then it will take time. Abraham certainly had to wait to receive what you had promised. But he trusted you, and even in the waiting he learned so much about you. Your Word says that "Abraham waited patiently, and he received what God had promised."[2] Patience is all about being able to wait for one reason: because we *trust* you.

And how can I be sure you want to grow this fruit of patience in me, Lord? Because the Bible reminds me "how wonderfully kind, tolerant, and patient"[3] you are toward us. Patience is so very much a part of your own character that you cannot fail to share it with those who draw close to you and seek it.

So Lord, please help me to patiently wait for patience; and as I do, to expect you to grow it in me, because that is what you've promised. Put me in situations today where this fruit has even more of a chance to grow! *Amen.*

---

[1] Galatians 5:22   [2] Hebrews 6:15   [3] Romans 2:4

Be still in the presence of the LORD,
and wait patiently for him to act.

PSALM 37:7

TRILLIUM
Thirty-nine native trilliums
grow in the United States.
Great white trillium is one of
the most common spring
wildflowers in eastern North
American woodlands.

LEARNING THROUGH

Failure

Learn to do good. ISAIAH 1:17

Lord, I LIKE TO GET THINGS RIGHT THE FIRST TIME. I hate not succeeding—I feel dumb and embarrassed. A failure. And I often feel that way in my walk with you. I fail you so much—sometimes through disobedience or fear; sometimes because I'm not as radical as I should be; sometimes because I'm trying to serve two masters. And then I feel useless because I hate failing.

But I'm not alone. Jesus' disciples failed . . . they failed *him*. They didn't always understand what he said; they didn't always use his power—and even when they did, it wasn't always in the right way or with the right attitude. They failed him at a crucial moment, fleeing when he was arrested in Gethsemane.[1] Not exactly a picture of first-time success.

And yet it strikes me that discipleship by its very nature must involve failure because discipleship is about learning—learning to live differently, learning to say no to things that I once loved and yes to what you want instead. And learning means I won't always get things right the first time, for discipleship is a process. The very word *disciple* means a learner or an apprentice. An apprentice comes alongside someone to learn their skills by watching, trying, failing, trying again, and eventually succeeding. And that's what Jesus wants for his followers, Lord.

---

[1] Matthew 26:56

So today I affirm that being a disciple will mean failing at times, but I resolve to let every failure be the seedbed of success for my next attempt. Thank you for giving me the space to fail so that you can train me to succeed. *Amen.*

Simon, Simon, Satan has asked to sift each of you like wheat. But I have pleaded in prayer for you, Simon,

that your faith should not fail.

LUKE 22:31-32

WINTER ACONITE
Winter aconite is a late-winter bloomer with buttercup-shaped, yellow blossoms. It's a European native, from France to Bulgaria, and blooms even before crocuses.

AN
Undivided Heart

I will give them singleness of heart and put a new spirit within them.
I will take away their stony, stubborn heart and give them a tender,
responsive heart, so they will obey my decrees and regulations. Then
they will truly be my people, and I will be their God. EZEKIEL 11:19-20

Lord, **THE WORLD WE LIVE IN** is a tough place, with all
sorts of things that aren't good or godly. Sometimes the gossip,
criticism, bad language, and bad attitudes have a way of getting
into my heart. There's stuff in my own life that finds a cozy corner
in my heart too—worries about today, unresolved issues from the
past, fears about the future. And then my heart gets cool, hard,
unresponsive, divided.

That's when I need you to fulfill the promise you made through
Ezekiel: to take away my stony, stubborn heart and replace it with
one that is soft, tender, and responsive to your Spirit. Yes, I know
that happens when I trust in Christ. But Lord, there are times when
I need you to fix my heart all over again—because if my heart is
divided, my mind will be too. And when I'm double-minded, I end
up adrift and tossed about in the uncertain seas of life, swayed by
this pressure and that pressure, by this opinion and that opinion,
by my will and your will.

So today, I invite you to do open-heart surgery on me; to remove
what needs removing and to renew what needs renewing, in order
that my heart may be soft and sensitive both to you and to your
people. *Amen.*

You must always act in the fear of the LORD,

with faithfulness and

an undivided heart.

2 CHRONICLES 19:9

BLUE SAGE

Blue sage, a hardy late
bloomer, is native to America's
western and southern prairies
but is also widely found across
the rest of the nation.

to Pray

Once Jesus was in a certain place praying. As he finished, one of his disciples came to him and said, "Lord, teach us to pray." LUKE 11:1

Lord, I SO EASILY IDENTIFY WITH JESUS' DISCIPLES— especially their mistakes and slowness to understand. And I can certainly identify with how they felt when, having seen him praying, they asked him to teach *them* how to pray.

Of course, it wasn't that they hadn't prayed before or didn't know how to; as Jews, they knew and said many prayers. But Jesus seemed to have a completely different way of praying. He made it look so easy, so desirable, so enjoyable! And the disciples wanted that for themselves, so he taught them what has become one of the most precious prayers in the world—the Lord's Prayer.

Yes, it's a prayer that I can repeat and pray—though since Jesus taught it in the context of warning us not to fall into mindless repetition, I need to be careful it doesn't become just a kind of mantra. But since it's also a pattern I can follow, help me to use it as a foundation for expanding my prayers.

So Lord, teach me to pray. Show me how to pray and what to pray for. Keep me from mindless ritual and empty words, and help me to simply talk to you about the things that matter in life, just like Jesus did. *Amen.*

Keep on asking, and you will receive what you ask for.

Keep on seeking, and you will find.

Keep on knocking, and the door will be opened to you.

For everyone who asks, receives.

Everyone who seeks, finds.

And to everyone who knocks,

the door will be opened.

LUKE 11:9-10

FORGET-ME-NOT

The forget-me-not flower is rich in symbolism for reasons related to loyalty or undying love. Its Greek name, *myosotis*, means "mouse's ear."

OUR FATHER

in Heaven . . .

Our Father in heaven . . .   MATTHEW 6:9

Lord, **THANK YOU FOR THIS REMINDER** that when I start to pray, I need to start not with me but with you. That's because when I start by focusing on what you are like, then everything else starts to take on its proper perspective. It sounds so obvious really, but I often forget!

When I start by focusing on myself, I can so quickly get discouraged, because my sin rises up to accuse me and tell me that I have no right to come to you or ask for anything. And if I start with my needs, I quickly get overwhelmed, for they are often so great and can seem so insoluble.

But when I start with you, my eyes are lifted up as I remember what a very big God you are!

Thank you, too, for the reminder that I don't need to address you as God in a general way. Jesus tells me to start by remembering that you are a God who is also my *Father*. And not just my Father, but my Father *in heaven*—that is, one without any of the limitations or restraints that this world brings. A Father without limits!

Lord, when I call on you as Father, prayer is transformed from a routine ritual into an exciting relationship and adventure. So I set my heart on you today as my Father, and I choose to see everything else in the light of that. *Amen.*

I thought to myself, "I would love to treat you as my own children!" I wanted nothing more than to give you this beautiful land—the finest possession in the world. I looked forward to your calling me "Father,"

and I wanted you never to turn from me.

JEREMIAH 3:19

CRIMSON BEE BALM

Crimson bee balm is part of the mint family. Native to the lower forty-eight states, it isn't found in Hawaii or Alaska.

KEEPING
God's Name Holy

May your name be kept holy.   MATTHEW 6:9

Lord, **THANK YOU FOR THIS REMINDER** from Jesus that your name is to be kept holy, honored, and hallowed, because your name tells us far more than who you are—it tells us what you are like and how we are to respond.

In Bible times, a name went far beyond distinguishing one person from another; it summed up someone's character or calling. That's why you changed the name of Abram ("exalted father") to "Abraham"[1]—to reflect what you were about to do for him and through him. It's why his son was called Isaac ("he laughs")[2]—as a reminder that Sarah, his wife, laughed with disbelief when you promised him to them, but then laughed with joy when she finally held him in her arms. A name says so much.

And likewise, *your* name speaks volumes about who you are. As Jesus reminded us, you are, first and foremost, a *Father*—so help me always to begin with that. But you are also a God of many names: El-Shaddai ("God Almighty"), El-Olam ("Eternal God"), El-Roi ("The God Who Sees Me"), Yahweh-Yireh ("The Lord Will Provide"), Yahweh-Shalom ("The Lord Is Peace"), Yahweh-Rophi ("The Lord Who Heals Me"). Lord, these names, and many more, remind me of how very great you are!

So I gladly honor your name today and will seek to keep it holy by living in the light of all you are and all you call me to be. May your name be kept holy in my life. *Amen.*

---

[1] See the footnote for Genesis 17:5, NLT   [2] See the footnote for Genesis 21:6, NLT

All praise to God, the Father of our Lord Jesus Christ, who has blessed us with every spiritual blessing in the heavenly realms because we are united with Christ.

EPHESIANS 1:3

ALPINE ASTER

The alpine aster resembles a pink, blue, purple, or white daisy and has a similar yellow-orange center. It doesn't like too much heat or humidity.

THE COMING OF
God's Kingdom

May your Kingdom come soon. MATTHEW 6:10

Lord, **WE DON'T OFTEN THINK ABOUT** your Kingdom; and yet it lay at the very heart of Jesus' message. It's even how he started his ministry as he went out preaching: "The time promised by God has come at last! . . . The Kingdom of God is near! Repent of your sins and believe the Good News!"[1]

In him, your Kingdom had truly come—in fact, every part of his life, especially his teachings and miracles, shouted the message that your kingly rule was breaking into this world. And wherever that rule was received, things changed! Yet Jesus tells us to pray for even more of that Kingdom—more of your kingly rule. For when there is more of your rule, we experience "a life of goodness and peace and joy in the Holy Spirit."[2]

So Lord, help me to pray, "May your Kingdom come soon," starting with my own life and working outward, like ripples from a stone dropped into a pond. Help me to have more of your kingly rule by seeking your will in everything—and then quickly doing it. Then help me to ask for more of your kingly rule over my family and friends, my church and its leaders, my work and my workplace, my city and its officials, my nation and its leaders, and my world and all that happens there.

Lord, let your Kingdom come! And let it start with me. *Amen*.

---

[1] Mark 1:15   [2] Romans 14:17

Since we are receiving a Kingdom that is unshakable,
let us be thankful and please God by worshiping him with

holy fear and awe.

HEBREWS 12:28

FRENCH MULBERRY

French mulberry, or American
beautyberry, is native to the
southeastern United States.
Native Americans used it
medicinally to treat fevers,
dysentery, and other
ailments.

DOING
God's Will

May your will be done on earth, as it is in heaven.   MATTHEW 6:10

Lord, **I REALLY LIKE THE IDEA** of your will being done. I think if everyone played their part, then the world would be a much better place. Of course, this gets more challenging when it's my turn to do your will. That's when, if I'm honest, I try to make excuses at times.

Yet I can't pray for your will to be done on earth if I'm not prepared to have it start with me. But as I grow in my trust and confidence in you, Father, that's not a difficult thing to do, for you always want my best. And Jesus himself set an example for me in Gethsemane when he prayed, "My Father! If it is possible, let this cup of suffering be taken away from me. Yet I want your will to be done, not mine."[1] He knew that your will is always a good will, from a good God, and since he knew he could trust you, I know I can too.

So I'll pray for your will to increasingly be done in my own life; for as I see your will accomplished "in here," I have confidence to pray that it will also be accomplished "out there"—in my family, city, nation, and world. And you also want us to pray that your will is done "on earth, as it is in heaven." And how is it done in heaven? Joyfully! Instantly! Willingly! Powerfully! Righteously! So Lord, may those qualities increasingly characterize my obedience. *Amen.*

---
[1] Matthew 26:39

We ask God to give you complete knowledge of his will and to give you spiritual wisdom and understanding.

COLOSSIANS 1:9

CALIFORNIA POPPY

The California poppy is California's state flower. It doesn't contain opium like its cousin the opium poppy, but it may help with insomnia and relaxation.

Present Needs

Give us today the food we need. MATTHEW 6:11

Lord, I LOVE HOW JESUS WAS SO PRACTICAL. He never dismissed our physical needs or saw them as less important than spiritual ones; he just told us to get them in the right perspective. And that's why the Lord's Prayer begins with a focus on you and not us. Yet once you are at the center, we can openly and honestly bring our needs to you, confident that you, our heavenly Father, really do want to hear our requests and answer us. And Jesus couldn't have started with a more practical need than food—our "daily bread."[1]

I'm encouraged that Jesus was saying our relationship with you is so deep, so intimate, so personal, that even the most basic necessities of daily life can be brought to you, whether food or any other need we might have. Nothing is too small or insignificant! I love the apostle Paul's encouragement: "Don't worry about *anything*; instead, pray about *everything*. Tell God what you need, and thank him for all he has done."[2]

So thank you, Lord, that I can confidently bring every need to you—material, financial, physical, relational, emotional, spiritual. Whatever it is, I refuse to think you are too busy to listen or too unconcerned to care. I'm asking with faith and expectation, knowing that Jesus has promised that you, my heavenly Father, really do care enough to want to provide. *Amen.*

---

[1] Matthew 6:11, KJV [2] Philippians 4:6, emphasis added

Give me neither poverty nor riches!

Give me just enough to satisfy my needs.

PROVERBS 30:8

POLYGALA

Polygala has been called a
superherb with significant
potential health benefits. It's said
to help depression, memory,
sleep, and cognitive abilities
in the elderly.

Past Sin

Forgive us our sins, as we have forgiven those who sin against us.

MATTHEW 6:12

Lord, I NEVER CEASE TO BE AMAZED at how you do things so differently than we do. Because if I'd written the Lord's Prayer, I'd have started by having people confess their sins right up front. But here it is, coming toward the end of the prayer!

Of course, Jesus knew there is a very real place for coming clean and confessing our sins. It's just that he said we shouldn't *start* there! He knew that if we did, we'd just dig a deeper hole for ourselves and end up in misery (and the devil would be happy to help us along the way). So Jesus told us not to start with our sin, but with you.

This instinctively cuts across everything within me! But it's because once we've seen how big, how gracious, how loving a Father you are, then we will be certain that you really do want to forgive us! And then admitting our failings won't seem half so difficult. We'll be able to confidently bring our sins to you, knowing that you will forgive them.

And we'll be just as confident in being able to forgive others, because we know that's what your loving and gracious nature requires of us. Indeed, if we don't forgive, we may question whether we really know what it is to be forgiven.

So today, Lord, help me to both forgive and be forgiven.

Amen.

If we claim we have no sin, we are only fooling ourselves and not living in the truth. But if we confess our sins to him, he is faithful and just to forgive us our sins and to *cleanse us from all wickedness.*

1 JOHN 1:8-9

INDIAN PAINTBRUSH

Indian paintbrush's fiery blossoms can be spotted throughout western parts of North and South America. One variety even grows in northwestern Russia's Kola Peninsula.

Future Welfare

Don't let us yield to temptation, but rescue us from the evil one.

MATTHEW 6:13

Lord, **THE DEVIL LOVES TO DECEIVE YOUR PEOPLE.** Just like he did with Adam and Eve, he tempts us to disobey you by dangling in front of us what is forbidden, always making it seem better than it really is. Little wonder he is called "the tempter."[1] He tempts because he loves to exploit our human weaknesses, making sin seem attractive and fooling us into thinking everything will be okay (even though experience cries out that it has never been okay when we've done it in the past).

But while the devil is powerful, I declare today that he is not *all*-powerful. Only you are, Lord! And Jesus proved this in his own life when the devil tempted him during those forty days in the wilderness. Each time, Jesus overcame by simply quoting from your powerful Word. Then he demonstrated his victory again and again by rescuing people from the devil's grip. And even though the devil thought he had triumphed when Jesus was nailed to the cross on Good Friday, you showed your ability to rescue him on Easter Sunday. What a shock the devil must have had that day!

So Father, I thank you that you are well able to protect me from all the attacks, accusations, and temptations of the evil one, whatever form they take. I may be weak before him—but you aren't! As I go through this day, I will take hold of that truth afresh. *Amen.*

---

[1] I Thessalonians 3:5

I'm not asking you to take them out of the world,

but to keep them safe from the evil one.

JOHN 17:15

BLUEBELL

Bluebells grow abundantly in the UK, where in Elizabethan times they were used to provide starch for clothing. Prolific bluebells signal an old woodland.

THE WHISPER OF
His Power

His Spirit made the heavens beautiful, and his power pierced the gliding serpent. These are just the beginning of all that he does, merely a whisper of his power. JOB 26:13-14

Lord, WHENEVER I SEE A SUNSET, I am amazed by the kaleidoscope of colors splashed across the sky, as though the heavens were on fire or some abstract painter had thrown his colors onto the cosmic canvas.

Little wonder Job spoke like he did. For even in the midst of all his troubles, he couldn't get away from the wonders of your creation. And as he surveyed them—the mystery of a sky held up by nothing; of clouds full of water yet not bursting under its weight; the beauty of the moon; the horizon that separates sky and oceans; the boundaries of light and dark; the mysteries of the ocean; the beauty of the skies—he stood in awe. And then he said, "These are just the beginning of all that he does, merely a whisper of his power."

What we can see is just the beginning, just a whisper, the mere outer fringe. Little wonder he stood in awe. Not all the scientific explanations in the world can rob us of that awe. And the more we discover, the more there is to be in awe of, whether in the depths of the ocean or the depths of the cosmos. And when we've finished marveling at our discoveries, they are still only a whisper of your power, for we haven't even begun to scratch the surface of your mysteries.

So Lord, I look—and stand in awe. *Amen.*

You alone are the LORD.
You made the skies and the heavens and all the stars.

*You made the earth and
the seas and everything in them.*

NEHEMIAH 9:6

BLUE CORNFLOWER
Native European blue
cornflower, or bachelor button,
grows widely across the United
States. Its vibrant blooms are
magnets for birds such as
American goldfinches.

BIG HEART,
Big Vision

People from nations and cities around the world will travel to Jerusalem. The people of one city will say to the people of another, "Come with us to Jerusalem to ask the LORD to bless us."

ZECHARIAH 8:20-21

Lord, HOW BIG THE PROPHETS' VISION WAS! They looked beyond the need for deliverance from their immediate circumstances to the greater deliverance that the Messiah would one day bring—not just for your own people but also for all the nations. A deliverance that would see them eager to come into your presence. And this at a time when those nations were opposing you! I'm challenged by such bigheartedness.

Jesus was bighearted too. For all sorts of people could sit in his presence—so much so that the religious dismissed him as "a friend of tax collectors and other sinners!"[1] And he sent his disciples to "go and make disciples of all the nations."[2] What a big heart! A heart not just for his own people, but for everyone, for all are made in your image, and all can respond to the gospel. That's why John could see gathered around your throne "a vast crowd, too great to count, from every nation and tribe and people and language, standing in front of the throne and before the Lamb."[3]

So Lord, forgive the smallness of my own heart. It too often thinks only of my own family, city, or nation—while your heart is for the whole world! Change my small thinking, Lord, and expand my heart. *Amen*.

---

[1] Matthew 11:19 [2] Matthew 28:19 [3] Revelation 7:9

People from many nations will come and say,
"Come, let us go up to the mountain of
the LORD, to the house of Jacob's God.
There he will teach us his ways,
and we will walk in his paths."

MICAH 4:2

EDELWEISS

Edelweiss is a mountain flower that loves rocky lime-stone heights. It was made popular in a song written for *The Sound of Music*.

Always There

I will not abandon you as orphans—I will come to you. JOHN 14:18

Lord, KNOWING SOMEONE IS *THERE* makes such a difference. For a young mother giving birth, an old person dying, a child learning to ride a bike—having someone there is so reassuring at such times. *Being there* makes all the difference.

Lord, it's good to know that you are always there too. Yes, you are "out there," sustaining the whole created universe; but you're also right here with me, moment by moment, day by day. What an amazing God!

But you're not only there for me; you are *always* there for me. And not only are you always there for me; you are also always there for me as a friend—a friend who will never leave me, never let me down, never give up on me.

I think of how Jesus' disciples started to get anxious when he began talking about leaving them. How would they cope without their friend? And that's when he made this promise: "I will not abandon you as orphans—I will come to you." They didn't know what he meant, of course; but now we know he was looking ahead to Pentecost, when he would baptize them with his Holy Spirit. Through this life-giving and empowering experience, they would know that Jesus was truly "there"—not limited by space or time or circumstances, but with each one of them forever, wherever they went, through the power of the Holy Spirit.

So Lord, I thank you for the promise that I have not been abandoned as an orphan, and that through your Holy Spirit you are absolutely here with me today. *Amen.*

I will live among the Israelites and
will never abandon my people Israel.
1 KINGS 6:13

DOG VIOLET
Unlike other violets, the
dog violet has no scent.
The Irish word for this flower
is *salchuach*, meaning
"cuckoo's heel."

AN ENCOUNTER
with Holiness

It's all over! I am doomed, for I am a sinful man. I have filthy lips, and I live among a people with filthy lips. Yet I have seen the King, the LORD of Heaven's Armies. ISAIAH 6:5

Lord, **THERE ARE THINGS IN LIFE** I try to avoid. Sometimes they're simple—like those jobs I really hate doing. But sometimes they're deeper things, where digging too deep might reveal issues I have to deal with.

And one of those deeper things I try to avoid, Lord, is your holiness. For I fear what I might be confronted with if I face up to it. Yet while at first Isaiah thought encountering your holiness would kill him, he discovered it was in fact the very thing that turned his life around.

His encounter with your holiness did two things. First, it revealed his sinfulness, for your holiness shows us what is wrong in our lives; and our initial response, like Isaiah's, is to withdraw—to cry, "It's all over!" But that's not where you left him. For the second thing his encounter with your holiness did was to bring your cleansing. Your holiness doesn't stand far off, accusing us; it takes action to come and cleanse and change us. For as the burning coal touched his lips, he was forgiven—and not only forgiven, but also commissioned to go as your messenger.[1]

So Lord, I thank you that you not only reveal my sin, but you also come to deal with it. Your holiness is only ever here to do me good! *Amen.*

---

[1] Isaiah 6:6-8

Set yourselves apart to be holy,

for I am the LORD your God. Keep all my decrees by putting them into practice, for I am the LORD who makes you holy.

LEVITICUS 20:7-8

AFRICAN DAISY
African daisies are native to South Africa and can be found in several unique varieties, including at least one with a blue center.

PUT YOUR

Belt On

Stand your ground, putting on the belt of truth. EPHESIANS 6:14

Lord, I LIVE IN A CULTURE where there is often little regard for truth. People don't think twice about things like bending the rules and telling "little white lies." Truth takes second place to need. And if I challenged others about this, they would think I was weird. But your Word tells us that truth is foundational to how you want us to live and a way of life that leads to blessing. Truth must take first place.

And that's what hit Paul as he sat in jail, looking at his Roman guard. He suddenly heard you speaking through what he saw and realized that as surely as the soldier had to put his armor on, so do your people. And then he told us to "put on all of God's armor"[1]—the first piece of which is the belt. The Roman soldier put this on first so that he could tuck his long garment into it. Next he tightened the buckle so there would be no danger of his garment tripping him up as he went into battle.

And that's what you want for us, Lord. You want us to ensure that the first thing in place is truth. For unless I am a person of truth, integrity, honesty, and sincerity—a person of my word—then I will most certainly get tripped up in life. And when that happens, it will open the door to the devil's accusations, ruin my testimony, and rob me of your blessing.

So today, help me to check that truth is in place, in every aspect of my life. *Amen.*

---

[1] Ephesians 6:11

People with integrity walk safely,
but those who follow crooked paths will be exposed.

PROVERBS 10:9

CHICORY
The leaves and roots of the
herbaceous chicory are edible.
Mixing them with other greens
in salads helps to mellow
their strong flavor.

EXTERNALS AND
Internals

> *The LORD doesn't see things the way you see them. People judge by outward appearance, but the LORD looks at the heart.* 1 SAMUEL 16:7

Lord, THERE IS PRESSURE ALL AROUND ME. Pressure to look good: to keep up with the latest fashions and wear the right outfits and labels. Pressure to keep the home looking perfect. Pressure to be seen with the right people or in the right places. But all these are externals. And you say that what matters is not external; what matters to you is *the heart*.

Even Samuel forgot this when looking for King Saul's replacement. Under pressure from the people and wanting to get things right, he was swayed by what he saw. After all, David's brother Eliab looked like such a fine candidate. But then you reminded Samuel that while people judge by outward appearance, you look only at the person's heart. And that's why Samuel had told Saul, "Your kingdom must end, for the LORD has sought out a man after his own heart."[1]

I know that having a good heart isn't about being perfect. After all, David, whom you pointed out to Samuel as your future chosen king, failed dismally many times in life. No, having a good heart is about knowing that the inside matters more than the outside, and then letting you in to deal with it, just as David did.

So in this world that prioritizes how things look on the outside, help me to remember that the most important thing to you is always my heart. *Amen*.

---

[1] 1 Samuel 13:14

Search me, O God, and know my heart; test me and know my anxious thoughts. Point out anything in me that offends you, *and lead me along the path of everlasting life.*

PSALM 139:23-24

YELLOW ROCKET

Yellow rocket, a weed that can be invasive, is often mistaken for wild mustard and wild radish.

FAITH IS NOT
a Commodity

*It was by faith that Abraham obeyed when God called him
to leave home and go to another land that God would
give him as his inheritance.* HEBREWS 11:8

Lord, PEOPLE SOMETIMES SPEAK ABOUT FAITH in ways that make my own faith seem so small. For them, it's almost as if faith is something that drops out of heaven and lifts them to a higher spiritual plane.

But that doesn't seem quite right to me, because faith isn't a *commodity*; it's a *relationship*—a relationship of daily trust as I walk with you, believing your promises to me and seeking to respond to them. When I look in your Word, I see that whenever you called people to have faith, it wasn't a call just to "faith"; it was always a call to have faith *in* you *for* something—and that "something" was always very specific.

When you revealed yourself to Abraham, what was it that you asked him to believe? Something very specific and tangible. You told him to look at the stars in the sky and promised him, "That's how many descendants you will have!"[1] And he believed you—despite circumstances that seemed hopeless from a human point of view. He wasn't vaguely hoping; his faith was in the specific promise that you made. And armed with that, he started a journey of faith that led to the promised blessing.

So today, Lord, I don't want to vaguely hope for things. Because of my relationship with you, I want to take hold of your specific promises—and believe. *Amen.*

---

[1] Genesis 15:5

It was by faith that even Sarah was able to have a child, though she was barren and was too old.

She believed that God would keep his promise.

HEBREWS 11:11

WILD BLEEDING HEART
Wild bleeding heart grows well alongside other shady plants, such as hostas. More compact than the pink bleeding heart, its multiple blooms are spectacular.

AT THE
Breaking Point

I can't carry all these people by myself! The load is far too heavy!
If this is how you intend to treat me, just go ahead and kill me.
Do me a favor and spare me this misery! NUMBERS 11:14-15

Lord, SOMETIMES I FEEL I'm at my breaking point. Life just crowds in—home, work, family, church, friends, finances—and I have no capacity for anything else. And then something else comes along. I could scream!

It's good to remember there are people in your Word who felt like that—like Moses did as he led the Israelites to the Promised Land. Desert life proved hard, so it wasn't long before they were grumbling and wishing they were back in Egypt.

When all this became too much for Moses, he hit his breaking point. But rather than putting his head down to keep going, he came to you, sharing both the problem and exactly how he felt. And he let you have it with both barrels! He asked why you had brought all this trouble his way; what he'd done to displease you; why he should care about your people anyway; how on earth you expected him to feed them all; how he was expected to bear their constant complaining. Little wonder he ended his prayer with the words in today's opening Scripture.

But you didn't rebuke him. You knew he was at his breaking point, so you provided a very practical solution. Since Moses had made himself indispensable, you simply told him to share the load a little. I love how practical you are, Lord!

74

So today, I stop—and bring everything to you. Tell me what to do with it, Lord—and I'll do it. *Amen.*

My enemies did their best to kill me,

but the LORD rescued me.

PSALM 118:13

WOOD VIOLET
Cherokee tribes treated colds and headaches with wood violet. Other violet varieties hold the title of state flower in New Jersey, Illinois, Wisconsin, and Rhode Island.

SAYING
I'm Sorry

I confess my sins; I am deeply sorry for what I have done.

PSALM 38:18

Lord, **SAYING I'M SORRY** is one of the hardest things for the human race to do. We see it in children, when trying to get them to say it can be such a battle. But actually, we adults aren't much better. We try to forget about the issue, change the topic, carry on as though nothing has happened—anything rather than just saying, "Sorry!"

But your Word reminds me that saying I'm sorry is so important. First, because it reminds me *who you are*: a holy God. You are sickened by sin—even by what I might see as trivial sin; for sin offends your holiness and breaks relationship. And owning up to sin is the first step toward seeing that relationship restored.

Second, because it reminds me *who I am*. I so easily lose a proper perspective and can convince myself of how right I am. But owning up to my sin makes me see things as they really are, and myself as I really am—a sinner just like others.

Third, because it reminds me *who others are*. Sometimes I hurt them with careless words, thoughtless actions, and ungrateful attitudes. But they are made in your image and therefore deserve to be respected. So owning up to my sin reminds me of that.

Saying I'm sorry isn't always easy. But help me today to say it quickly, both to you and to others. For when I do, it is the most liberating thing on earth! *Amen.*

Finally, I confessed all my sins to you
and stopped trying to hide my guilt.
I said to myself, "I will confess
my rebellion to the LORD."
And you forgave me!

*All my guilt
is gone.*

PSALM 32:5

JACOB'S LADDER
The blooms of Jacob's ladder
are shaped like cups and grow in
loose clusters on the plant. They
attract butterflies and other
nectar-seeking insects.

WHAT'S IN IT
for Me?

He alone is your God, the only one who is worthy
of your praise.   DEUTERONOMY 10:21

Lord, **EVERYONE IS ALWAYS ASKING,** "What's in it for me?" Oh, they may not use those words; but it's what they mean. They'll happily do something—as long as they get something out of it. And such thoughts can creep into my own heart at times—which is why it's good for me to worship. Worship cuts across this utilitarian instinct, for worship promises nothing for me; it is something given solely to you.

It's not that you need my worship in any way. You aren't made any less if I don't worship you, and you aren't made any greater if I do. The fact that you don't need worship is shown in your Word by how you refused to accept worship at any price. When the people of Isaiah's day thought the mere externals of worship would keep you happy and on their side, you said, "When you come to worship me, who asked you to parade through my courts with all your ceremony? Stop bringing me your meaningless gifts; the incense of your offerings disgusts me!"[1] They were only interested in worship for what they could get out of it, not for what it gave you; so you told them very clearly what you thought.

What's in it for me? Nothing! Yet the mystery is that when I worship you, things happen to me and for me, for I am drawn into the sphere of your presence. So today, I worship you—not for what I can get out of it, but because you are worth it, Lord. *Amen.*

---

[1] Isaiah 1:12-13

78

He is God, the one who rules over everything and is worthy of eternal praise!

ROMANS 9:5

FOXGLOVE BEARDTONGUE

Foxglove beardtongue is named for the tuft of hairs on its stamen. It can grow diversely in prairies, floodplain forests, and even savannas.

Blame Shifting

O Israel, my faithless people, come home to me again,
for I am merciful. I will not be angry with you forever.
Only acknowledge your guilt. JEREMIAH 3:12-13

Lord, THERE'S SOMETHING IN ME that always wants to shift the blame. And when I do, I always feel better—at least for a few moments, because it removes the focus from me. But it's not long before the conscience that I had hoped to ease begins to nag away at me.

Blame shifting goes right back to Adam and Eve. When you challenged Adam about his disobedience, he immediately blamed it on his wife: "It was the woman you gave me who gave me the fruit, and I ate it." But Eve was ready with her excuses too. "The serpent deceived me," she said. "That's why I ate it."[1]

But Adam and Eve weren't the last. Aaron blamed the Israelites for leading him into idolatry;[2] Saul blamed his soldiers' fears for his disobedience to Samuel's command;[3] Martha blamed Jesus for Lazarus's death because he failed to arrive on time.[4] Blame shifting is characteristic of the fallen human race.

Why do we do it? Sometimes because of pride, for we want to look good and don't want to admit we've made a mistake; and sometimes because of fear, for we worry about the consequences of owning up to what we've done and hope that somehow it will all turn out okay.

But blame shifting is the one thing that puts us outside your grace; for grace can be found only when we own up to our sin. So today, Lord, please help me not to shift blame. *Amen.*

---

[1] Genesis 3:12-13   [2] Exodus 32:22-23   [3] 1 Samuel 13:5-12   [4] John 11:21

LORD, we confess our wickedness and that of our ancestors, too.
We all have sinned against you. For the sake of your reputation,
LORD, do not abandon us.

JEREMIAH 14:20-21

**WILD RED AND
WHITE TULIP**
The wild red and white tulip is a
"species tulip," typically smaller
and hardier than hybrids.
It loves dry sites with
good drainage.

Thirsty for God

As the deer longs for streams of water, so I long for you, O God.
I thirst for God, the living God. PSALM 42:1-2

Lord, **WHEN I'M REALLY THIRSTY**, there's nothing I wouldn't do for a long, cold, refreshing drink. It tastes so good! And that's how you want me to be with you: thirsty—really thirsty—for you, so that I drink of you until I'm satisfied and quench my thirst, knowing it's done me good.

That was the psalmist's experience. He was desperately thirsty for you, longing for you more than anything else. He wouldn't be satisfied until he'd drunk his fill. And when I read the verses above, I find it easy to say, "Yes, Lord! That's what I want too—to have that kind of thirst and find it quenched!"

But it comes with a price, because such thirst can grow only if I've settled my priorities. For although there are other important things in life I need to give myself to, you said my most important priority is to "seek the Kingdom of God above all else."[1] You want me to come to the point where I say, "You and you alone are the most important thing in life! You are what I'm most thirsty for. Everything else is insignificant compared to you."

And this means being ready to let go of things that have taken up the most precious places in my heart. So Lord, search my heart today and show me what I am truly thirsty for. *Amen.*

---

[1] Matthew 6:33

O God, you are my God; I earnestly search for you. My soul thirsts for you; my whole body longs for you in this parched and weary land where there is no water.

PSALM 63:1

PURPLE SWEET PEA
Purple sweet pea symbolizes delicate pleasure, departure, and gratitude for a lovely time. Its flowers make beautiful additions to wedding decor.

Unanswered Prayer

Three different times I begged the Lord to take it away.
Each time he said, "My grace is all you need. My power
works best in weakness." 2 CORINTHIANS 12:8-9

Lord, I STRUGGLE WITH why you don't always answer prayer. I'm sure I'm not on my own in this. In fact, Paul brought the same question to you. And when he did, you gave him the answer: because you were doing something bigger and better than he could ever have imagined. He just couldn't see it at the time.

Sometimes it's simply because you know more than we do, and that keeps you from answering—like when Job didn't know there was something far more important going on than his life becoming comfortable again.[1] Sometimes it's because the timing isn't right—like when Mary and Martha asked Jesus to come and heal Lazarus, and Jesus didn't respond immediately because he knew you had planned a greater miracle.[2]

Sometimes it's because we simply don't understand your bigger plan—like when Joseph couldn't be released from jail until just the right moment so your people could be saved.[3] Sometimes it's because we simply ask for the wrong things, or ask for the right things but with wrong motives—and you are always far more interested in our hearts than anything else.[4] And sometimes it's because we simply don't have faith,[5] or because our sin is blocking you from working.[6]

---

[1] Job 1:8-12 [2] John 11:2-4 [3] Genesis 41:14-37 [4] James 4:3 [5] Matthew 13:53-58 [6] Isaiah 59:2

Lord, there are so many reasons. But perhaps the biggest reason is that you need to keep me humble, for if all my prayers were answered, I would probably be unbearable. So when my prayers aren't being answered, keep me humble, keep me patient, and keep me trusting in you. *Amen*.

Wait patiently for the LORD. Be brave and courageous. Yes, wait patiently for the LORD.

PSALM 27:14

SNOWDROP

Snowdrop flowers look like small, drooping, delicate white bells. In some regions they emerge in February or March, even through snow cover.

THE GOD OF
Flesh and Blood

*Because God's children are human beings—made of flesh and blood—
the Son also became flesh and blood. For only as a human being could
he die, and only by dying could he break the power of the devil,
who had the power of death.* HEBREWS 2:14

Lord, **TO THINK THAT YOU WOULD** become a human being!
Not some sort of half-god, half-man; not just pretending to be
human, but truly and fully human, "made of flesh and blood,"
just like us. How staggering!

So staggering that some of the first Christians struggled to
accept it. But John gave this testimony of his experience: "We
proclaim to you the one who existed from the beginning, whom
we have heard and seen. We saw him with our own eyes and
touched him with our own hands."[1]

Heard! Seen! Touched! Yes, there was no doubt that Jesus
was indeed a real man. And he did everything that characterizes
real human beings: getting tired, being thirsty, feeling hungry,
sleeping, feeling emotions, enjoying children, socializing, griev-
ing over a friend's death, suffering, and the ultimate human
experience—dying.

Lord, I am so encouraged by all this. For the fact that your Son
became truly "flesh and blood" means he can understand and
help me in every situation; because whatever I face, he himself
has faced. So Lord, I claim that help today. *Amen.*

---

[1] I John 1:1

It was necessary for him to be made in every respect like us, his brothers and sisters,

so that he could be our merciful and faithful High Priest before God. Then he could offer a sacrifice that would take away the sins of the people. Since he himself has gone through suffering and testing, he is able to help us when we are being tested.

HEBREWS 2:17-18

BALLOON VINE

"Love in a puff" is another name for the balloon vine, an edible but invasive weed. Its fruit looks like balloons or Chinese lanterns.

a Breakthrough

Since the first day you began to pray for understanding and to humble yourself before your God, your request has been heard in heaven. I have come in answer to your prayer. But for twenty-one days the spirit prince of the kingdom of Persia blocked my way. DANIEL 10:12-13

Lord, I SOMETIMES FORGET there's more to life than just what I can see. Things are often happening behind the scenes—not just the human scenes, "for we are not fighting against flesh-and-blood enemies, but against evil rulers and authorities of the unseen world, against mighty powers in this dark world, and against evil spirits in the heavenly places."[1]

That's why Daniel's prayers weren't answered—because there were spiritual hindrances. So I'm asking for your Spirit's help to really understand what's going on and engage in spiritual warfare to see the breakthroughs that I need.

But in your Word, Lord, spiritual warfare seems so . . . ordinary! It doesn't challenge us to identify demons and bind them up, but rather to pray and fast, like Daniel did;[2] to submit to you and see the devil flee;[3] to claim Christ's victory at the cross, where Satan and all his demons were stripped of power;[4] to change my ways of thinking that have become strongholds that need demolishing;[5] to return to my first love, as the church at Ephesus was called to do.[6]

Such "ordinary" things, Lord; but things you tell me will help

---

[1] Ephesians 6:12   [2] Daniel 10:1-19   [3] James 4:7   [4] Colossians 2:15   [5] 2 Corinthians 10:3-5   [6] Revelation 2:4-5

remove hindrances to my praying. Show me today which of these I need to embrace again in order to have my breakthrough. *Amen.*

Humble yourselves before God. Resist the devil, and he will flee from you.

JAMES 4:7

DENSE BLAZING STAR

The dense blazing star commonly grows two to four feet tall, but it can reach up to five or six feet. Bold purple flowers cover its stalk.

When You're Down

"I have had enough, LORD," [Elijah] said. "Take my life, for I am no better than my ancestors who have already died." 1 KINGS 19:4

Lord, SOMETIMES I REALLY FEEL DOWN, even depressed. I hardly dare to acknowledge it for fear some cheery friend will tell me, "Pull yourself together!" or ask, "Where's your faith?" But I've not stopped believing in you or trusting you; it's just that my mind and emotions are struggling to recover.

That's when it's good to think about the people in your Word who sometimes felt this way: Naomi, faced with destitution and so depressed that she changed her name from Naomi ("Pleasant") to Mara ("Bitter").[1] Hagar, so badly treated by Abram's wife that she ran away in despair.[2] Job, who despaired of life itself because of his sufferings.[3] Jeremiah, who was so depressed that he accused you of deceiving him.[4]

Sometimes it's easy to understand why we hit low points, and at others it isn't. Elijah had just experienced your tremendous victory over Baal's prophets but then fell apart completely when Jezebel threatened his life. He fled, collapsed, and told you he was ready to die.

But I'm encouraged you didn't rebuke him or try to fix him. You dealt with him tenderly: You gave him sleep, got him to eat, encouraged him to express his feelings, got him to do something practical—and only then sent him back to get on with life, reassuring him he was not alone.

[1] See the footnote for Ruth 1:20, NLT [2] Genesis 16:1-6 [3] Job 3:1-26 [4] Jeremiah 20:7

Thank you that just as you didn't rebuke Elijah, you will not rebuke me; so help me to always be honest with you about my feelings. *Amen.*

To all who mourn in Israel, he will give a crown of beauty for ashes, a joyous blessing instead of mourning, festive praise instead of despair.

ISAIAH 61:3

WILD BERGAMOT

Wild bergamot is also called bee balm and horsemint. Native to North America, it's been used in tea infusions for numerous medical issues.

Me, Me, Me . . .

Not to us, O LORD, not to us, but to your name goes all the glory for your unfailing love and faithfulness. PSALM 115:1

Lord, **THE SOCIETY I LIVE IN** is so utterly "me" oriented. All the advertising is about how *I* can feel better, look better, be better thought of. All the attitudes center on *my* rights and what *I* can get out of things. Even some worship songs are about *me* rather than *you*—about how I feel or what I want rather than what you are like or what you have done. Me, me, me . . .

I confess this sometimes spills over into my prayer life, Lord. It becomes all about me and my desires, with little space given to you. I rush into your presence with my list of requests, share them hastily with you—and then wonder why I don't sense your presence. I come away feeling empty, as if I had gone looking for you as my divine Santa Claus but was surprised to find you weren't home.

Which is why I need this psalmist's reminder that it's not about me; it's about you. It's why I need to remember how the prayer that Jesus taught us begins, "Our Father in heaven . . ."[1] Real prayer—engaging prayer, soul-moving prayer—begins with you, Lord . . . for starting with you puts things wonderfully in perspective. It reminds me that you are God, not me; that your will is what matters, not mine; that you should be at the center, not me.

So Lord, today help me to put you first in my prayers; to focus on you, your character, and your glory, and not on my needs.

Amen.

---

[1] Matthew 6:9

You must not have any other god but me.

NEW ENGLAND ASTER
New England asters, or
Michaelmas daisies, can grow up
to six feet tall. As late bloomers,
they're an important food
source for autumn
pollinators.

Far Away

My God, my God, why have you abandoned me?
Why are you so far away when I groan for help? Every day I call to
you, my God, but you do not answer. Every night I lift my voice,
but I find no relief. Yet . . . PSALM 22:1-3

Lord, AT TIMES I FEEL YOU ARE FAR AWAY. It's usually when some crisis happens, or when an ongoing situation has worn me down and my prayers just seem to hit the ceiling.

But I'm encouraged to know there were people in the Bible who felt the same way. People like David. He had certainly known your intimate presence; but when he wrote this psalm, he felt you were so far away, even that you had abandoned him and were no longer listening to his prayers.

But then that little word *yet* comes. Yes, he felt abandoned; and yet . . . he began to rehearse what he knew about you rather than what he was feeling at the moment. David declared all the "yets" of life—your faithfulness to your people over generations, your answering of their prayers, your care for him since his birth . . . and suddenly he found so many things to praise you for. His perspective began to change and his spirits began to lift as he set his eyes on you once again.

So Lord, when you seem far away, help me to declare all the "yets" of life and to focus on your promises rather than my feelings. *Amen*.

Don't be afraid, for I am with you.

Don't be discouraged, for I am your God. I will strengthen you and help you. I will hold you up with my victorious right hand.

ISAIAH 41:10

MOUNTAIN ANGELICA

Mountain angelica is endangered in Kentucky and Maryland. Its range in the Appalachian Mountains reaches from northeast Georgia through Pennsylvania.

the Spirit

Pray in the Spirit at all times and on every occasion.
Stay alert and be persistent in your prayers for all believers
everywhere. EPHESIANS 6:18

Lord, **IF I'M HONEST**, sometimes I find that praying is hard work. I start thinking of all the things I need to get done; or I don't know what I should pray for; or I get tired of praying the same thing. And then my mind wanders . . . which is why I suppose your Word tells us to "pray in the Spirit."

When we pray in our own efforts and energy, it's just hard work. But your Holy Spirit changes that by helping us in our weakness. We don't know what you want us to pray for, but the Holy Spirit prays for us with groanings that can't be expressed in words. And you know what the Spirit is saying, for the Spirit pleads for us believers in harmony with your own will.[1]

To think the Holy Spirit prays *for* me and *with* me! He prays *for* me, seeing my needs and bringing them before you, even when I struggle to put them into words! He prays *with* me by reminding me of my relationship with you, which is at the heart of why I pray; by convicting me of sin so nothing can hinder my prayers; by showing me your heart and truth so I can know better what to pray about; and by alerting me to the needs of others.

So help me today to pray in the Spirit and to trust the thoughts he drops into my mind, seeing them not as a distraction but as his promptings to pray. *Amen.*

---

[1] Personalized paraphrase of Romans 8:26-27

Pray in the power of the Holy Spirit.

JUDE 1:20

PITCHER PLANT
Carnivorous pitcher plants attract insects with the nectar inside their "pitcher" traps. They grow in permanently moist locations such as swamps, bogs, and riverbanks.

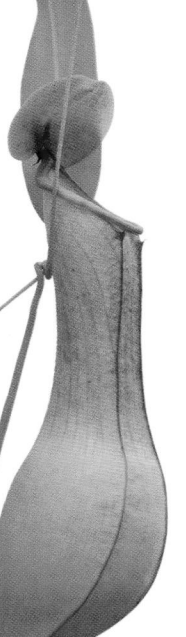

Just Stand!

Stay alert! Watch out for your great enemy, the devil. He prowls around like a roaring lion, looking for someone to devour. Stand firm against him, and be strong in your faith. 1 PETER 5:8-9

Lord, YOU CALL ME TO STAND—to stand firm not in who I am, but in who you are; not in what I have done, but in what you have done for me. Yet the devil doesn't like it when I stand. He tries to threaten me, intimidate me, scare me, browbeat me. And sometimes I'm foolish enough to let him.

But although Satan may be powerful, he's nowhere near as powerful as you! He is merely the created; you are the Creator. So I don't need to be afraid of him. And Christ stripped him of his power at the cross.

Yet Satan doesn't give up easily. He still "prowls around like a roaring lion, looking for someone to devour." But he's just a bully, wanting me to believe he has more power than he really does and trying to convince me that I must do what he wants.

So today, I take hold of your simple solution for dealing with any bully: standing up to him not in my own strength, but in yours—which is why James tells us, "Humble yourselves before God. Resist the devil, and he will flee from you."[1] And then I put on my spiritual armor: truth, righteousness, peace, preparedness, faith, assurance of salvation, and obedience to your Word.[2] With these things in place, all I need to do is . . . *stand!*

Lord, help me to do just that. *Amen.*

---

[1] James 4:7 [2] Ephesians 6:13-17

*Put on all of God's armor so
that you will be able to stand firm
against all strategies of the devil.*

EPHESIANS 6:11

BEARBERRY

Bearberry groundcover gets its
name because bears, along with
other wildlife, love its berries.
It thrives on the poor soil that
other plants don't enjoy.

THE LORD,

My Lover

His mouth is sweetness itself; he is desirable in every way.
Such, O women of Jerusalem, is my lover, my friend.

SONG OF SONGS 5:16

Lord, **I FIND MYSELF** almost shocked by these words. To think of you not just as my friend, but also as my lover, strikes an intimacy which is almost uncomfortable. We're so often encouraged to relate to you with our heads rather than our hearts, and to see emotion as belonging to the fringe of Christianity rather than at the center of it. Yet if your message is one of love, then surely it must touch the seat of love—my heart.

People have always struggled with the book of Song of Songs, haven't they? Many see it as just a set of love songs between a man and a woman, depicting love in all its power and wonder. But many others have also seen in it a beautiful parallel of the love between Christ and his church, underscoring how much he wants to be not just our Savior but also our lover. A lover is kind, generous, intimate, playful, supportive, unselfish, uninhibited, enthusiastic, mindful, confident, proud, and admiring. A lover is one's best friend.

Lord, may I grow in letting you be all these things to me. May I not restrict my relationship with you to one of head knowledge: knowing facts about you but not really knowing you; saying, "He loves me!" yet never really experiencing the feelings behind those words. Help me to let you be my lover. And help me to grow in being your lover too, so that I can truly say, "My lover is mine, and I am his."[1] *Amen.*

---

[1] Song of Songs 2:16

My lover said to me, "Rise up, my darling!

Come away with me, my fair one!"

SONG OF SONGS 2:10

LADY SLIPPER
Native American legend claims a brave maiden ran barefoot through snow to find medicine for her tribe. Lady slippers grew where she perished.

Complain to God!

O God, listen to my complaint. PSALM 64:1

Lord, I DON'T HESITATE TO COMPLAIN when I've received poor service; but the idea of complaining to you seems so inappropriate—and certainly dangerous. For your Word has stories of people who complained and received your judgment, like the Israelites in the wilderness who began to complain about their hardship. You heard everything they said and became angry, so you sent a fire among them and destroyed some of the people outside the camp.[1] Complaining looks pretty dangerous!

Yet your Word also contains many prayers of complaint: complaints about what you do, like Jonah complaining about Nineveh being spared;[2] complaints about how you work, like Moses complaining that being sent to Pharaoh was just making things worse;[3] complaints about what you don't do, like Habakkuk complaining that you were allowing evil to go unpunished.[4] Why did these people complain and get away with it, while others were punished?

But then I see that it was *how* they complained that made the difference. For our complaints shouldn't be *about* you, but *to* you. When we complain to *others*, we're really saying, "God, you don't know what you're doing, and I don't trust you!" But when we complain to *you*, we're saying, "God, I don't know what you are doing; but I really would like to!"

---

[1] Numbers 11:1 [2] Jonah 3:10—4:3 [3] Exodus 5:22-23 [4] Habakkuk 1:12-17

So help me to bring any complaints directly to you today, Lord. And as I do, make me ready to listen as you explain things from your point of view. *Amen.*

I will climb up to my watchtower and stand at my guardpost. There I will wait to see what the LORD says and how he will answer my complaint.

HABAKKUK 2:1

JACK-IN-THE-PULPIT
Raw parts of this unique-looking plant cause irritation if ingested or touched. But Native Americans enjoyed eating its roots, which are edible after cooking.

to Look

When I look at the night sky and see the work of your fingers—
the moon and the stars you set in place—what are mere mortals
that you should think about them, human beings that
you should care for them? PSALM 8:3-4

Lord, **DAVID WAS RIGHT!** We only have to look at the night sky to feel overwhelmed by the vastness of creation. All those stars! And even what we see is but a tiny handful of the millions and millions you have created. How small we are in comparison to it all—and yet how central!

But this psalm doesn't praise "nature"—for nature assumes it all came about "naturally"; and it didn't! It came about because you created it, Lord. Creation has a Creator! So when I look at it, it directs me to you.

The trouble is, Lord, I'm often so busy that I fail to stop and marvel at what you have created. I drive everywhere, so I whiz past what's around me. I hurry through crowds, so I don't take time to look at people's faces and the wondrous variety you have put in them. And even when I do stop and look, familiarity has caused me to lose a sense of wonder.

So Lord, help me today to stop rushing and start looking; and as I look, to wonder. To feel the breeze touch my skin, look at the stars, smell the air—and remember that you have made them all! *Amen*.

Ever since the world was created, people have seen the earth and sky. Through everything God made, they can clearly see his invisible qualities—his eternal power and divine nature.

So they have no excuse for not knowing God.

ROMANS 1:20

SWAMP MILKWEED

As its name suggests, swamp milkweed favors wetlands, flooded plains, marshes, and swamps. A soap-water spray relieves it of inevitable pesty insects.

THE GIFT
of Work

*To enjoy your work and accept your lot in life—this is indeed
a gift from God.* ECCLESIASTES 5:19

Lord, SOMETIMES WORK CAN BE SO HARD AND
FRUSTRATING—in the home, with the family, at the workplace—
and yet your Word reminds me that work is not a nuisance; it is
a blessing.

From the very beginning, you designed us to work. You put
Adam and Eve in the Garden and told them to "tend and watch
over it."[1] Your beautiful world wasn't going to look after itself;
you gave humanity the job of caring for it and bringing the best
out of it. And that means work. But this shouldn't surprise us, for
you yourself are a God who works, as we see at Creation. And
Jesus told us, "My Father is always working."[2] So since we're
made in your image, it shouldn't surprise us to find that we, too,
are designed to work.

Of course, after the Fall, sin spoiled everything, including work.
But it wasn't *work* that you cursed. You said, "The *ground* is cursed
because of you. All your life you will struggle to scratch a living from
it. . . . By the sweat of your brow will you have food to eat."[3] Work
became hard at times, and not always the joy it was meant to be.

So Lord, help me to remember that work isn't under your curse.

---

[1] Genesis 2:15   [2] John 5:17   [3] Genesis 3:17, 19, emphasis added

How can it be when it is your gift? But it can be demanding.
So please help me in my work today and bless all that I set my
hand to. *Amen.*

Make it your goal to live a quiet life, minding your own business
and working with your hands, just as we instructed you before.

1 THESSALONIANS 4:11

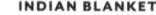

INDIAN BLANKET
Indian blanket's red petals
radiate from a large, colorful
center and end in brilliant yellow
tips. This flower is common
along roads in the
Southwest.

THE DESTRUCTIVE POWER
of Jealousy

Should you be jealous because I am kind to others? MATTHEW 20:15

Lord, THERE'S SOMETHING IN ME I really don't like—and I'm sure you don't like it either. I get resentful when others are blessed and I'm not; when they are thanked and I'm not; when they get a raise at work and I don't. Suddenly all sorts of feelings rise up in me—and they're not very pleasant.

What's even worse is when those same feelings arise about the *way* you bless others. Often they've been praying for years, and suddenly their prayers are answered—but the prayer I've been praying for years still isn't. Or they're given roles in the church that I would have loved. And suddenly, jealousy fills my heart.

But Lord, how unreasonable of me to complain about how you treat others. You can treat them however you want. You are, after all, God! So who am I to question you? You are the potter, and you can shape the clay into any form you choose.

And Lord, how foolish of me to complain that your dealings aren't fair. For if you treated any of us on the basis of what is fair, the only outcome is that we would all be condemned. But you are a God of mercy who doesn't give us what we deserve; rather, in your grace you give us more than we could ever deserve.

So free me today from the destructive power of jealousy. Help me to live in your abundant grace and to rejoice in the abundant grace that you show to others, too. *Amen.*

Jealousy and selfishness are not God's kind of wisdom.

Such things are earthly, unspiritual, and demonic.

JAMES 3:15

BLACKFOOT DAISY

"Blackfoot daisy" sounds like a cohort of Calamity Jane or Annie Oakley, but it's a Texas wildflower also found in five other southwestern states.

WORSHIP THAT
Releases Power

*At the very moment they began to sing and give praise,
the LORD caused the armies of Ammon, Moab, and Mount Seir
to start fighting among themselves.*   2 CHRONICLES 20:22

Lord, **I'M FASCINATED** by this story. King Jehoshaphat was surrounded by enemies, hopelessly outnumbered, and facing sure annihilation. And yet you sent a prophet to tell him and his people, "This is what the LORD says: Do not be afraid! Don't be discouraged by this mighty army, for the battle is not yours, but God's. . . . You will not even need to fight. Take your positions; then stand still and watch the LORD's victory."[1] So the next morning, the king sent out worshipers ahead of the soldiers. And as they began to worship, you did something amazing: You caused their enemies to start fighting one another. Such an amazing example of what praise can do!

And Jehoshaphat wasn't alone. For whenever your people set their hearts to worship you, there were always breakthroughs. Hindrances were removed, difficulties were overcome, problems were resolved, and enemies were defeated. But that worship wasn't half-hearted. It was full of passion, energy, commitment, faith—what older translations of the Old Testament call "the high praises of God."[2] For there are times when "ordinary praise" just won't do and we really need to give it all we've got—in volume,

---

[1] 2 Chronicles 20:15, 17   [2] Psalm 149:6, KJV

in passion, in faith, in the Spirit. And when we do, your people see breakthroughs.

So today, Lord, help me to set my heart on you and offer up my passionate worship, knowing that as I do, I can expect to see you act and will start to see breakthroughs in my own situation.

Amen.

I called on the LORD, who is worthy of praise,
and he saved me from my enemies.

2 SAMUEL 22:4

MOUNTAIN AVENS

White-blooming mountain avens is Iceland's national flower. It loves cold, sunny locations as far north as Alaska and Canada's Yukon and Northwest Territories.

In Anxious Times

Listen and answer me, for I am overwhelmed by my troubles. . . .
My heart pounds in my chest. . . . But I will call on God,
and the LORD will rescue me.   PSALM 55:2, 4, 16

Lord, **WE ALL GET ANXIOUS AT TIMES,** including me. This seems to be a very human experience, for in your Word there are many people who grappled with it, and there are also many encouragements not to worry.

But whatever my anxiety and whatever its cause, your Word teaches me to bring it to you, just as King David did. In Psalm 55, he didn't try to hide his feelings or pretend the anxiety wasn't there. He was real with you, even though he was so anxious that he wanted to run away from everything: "Oh, that I had wings like a dove; then I would fly away and rest!"[1]

But mixed with his anxiety were firm declarations of trust in you: "I will call on God, and the LORD will rescue me. Morning, noon, and night I cry out in my distress, and the LORD hears my voice. . . . I am trusting you to save me."[2] And despite everything, he gave us this strong encouragement: "Give your burdens to the LORD, and he will take care of you."[3]

So Lord, whatever my anxieties may be, help me to bring them honestly and openly to you and to believe, like David, that you have committed yourself to being faithful to me and to sustaining me until I come through. *Amen.*

---

[1] Psalm 55:6   [2] Psalm 55:16-17, 23   [3] Psalm 55:22

*Give all your worries and cares
to God, for he cares about you.*

1 PETER 5:7

CREEPING NAVELWORT
Creeping navelwort is also known as blue-eyed Mary, an alternate moniker that some may find much more flattering to this simple, cheery beauty.

HE NEVER
Gives Up

Oh, how can I give you up, Israel? How can I let you go? HOSEA 11:8

Lord, **I OFTEN FEEL LIKE GIVING UP**—not just on tasks, but sometimes on people, too. I always give my best effort; but when nothing seems to change, I just want to give up.

But I thank you today that you never feel like this. When you start something, you always finish it. You never give up, never stop trying to redeem what's lost, spoiled, or broken—including me. How can I be so confident of that? Because it has nothing to do with me; it's all about you from start to finish. For you made a covenant with us through your Son, Jesus. And because of this covenant, you remain faithful to us, even when we're unfaithful to you.[1]

But I know that the fact you show me such grace and faithfulness doesn't mean you let me get away with anything, like some weak father might do with his children. You love me far too much, which is why you promise to bring your tender discipline into my life when I need it. For you correct those you love, "just as a father corrects a child in whom he delights."[2]

So I thank you that you will never give up on me; and I also thank you that part of your not giving up means you will sometimes bring your loving discipline into my life. Help me to neither misinterpret nor reject that. *Amen.*

---

[1] 2 Timothy 2:13 [2] Proverbs 3:12

I am certain that God, who began the good work within you, will continue his work until it is finally finished on the day when Christ Jesus returns.

PHILIPPIANS 1:6

CLOVER

Clover, or trefoil, is a member of the pea family and is characterized by three leaflets and spiky white or red flowers.

PRAYING FOR

My Nation

Build homes, and plan to stay. . . . Work for the peace and prosperity of the city where I sent you into exile. Pray to the LORD for it, for its welfare will determine your welfare. JEREMIAH 29:5, 7

Lord, **I WANT TO SEE THE PEOPLE** in my nation blessed by you and living in more godly ways! I want to live in a nation full of righteousness and justice, where love for you and others is the norm rather than the exception. But if I'm honest, I seldom pray for that.

Yet your Word tells me to pray for my nation, even—especially—if it is godless. Through Jeremiah you told Israel to pray for godless Babylon, where they were exiled, and to seek its good; for in seeking its good, they would find their good.[1] Through Paul you told the church to pray for godless Rome and to submit to its rulers[2]—even though Nero was emperor and would soon persecute Christians; and Peter said the same thing.[3]

You didn't want your people retreating into their own little groups, leaving Babylon and Rome to their godless ways; rather, you told them to pray for those nations and to do all they could to bless them.

So help me not to grumble about my government but to pray for it—whether I voted for the current leaders or not, whether they represent my party or not. For if my nation is blessed, then I, too, will be blessed. *Amen.*

---

[1] Jeremiah 29:4-7   [2] Romans 13:1-5; 1 Timothy 2:1-4   [3] 1 Peter 2:13-17

I urge you, first of all, to pray for all people.

Ask God to help them; intercede on their behalf, and give thanks for them. Pray this way for kings and all who are in authority so that we can live peaceful and quiet lives marked by godliness and dignity. 1 TIMOTHY 2:1-2

PRICKLY PEAR
Several varieties of prickly pear cactus are part of the Mexican diet. It may decrease the absorption of sugar and cholesterol into the bloodstream.

for Me

*Simon, Simon, Satan has asked to sift each of you like wheat. But
I have pleaded in prayer for you, Simon, that your faith
should not fail.* LUKE 22:31-32

Lord, I OFTEN SAY TO PEOPLE, "I'll pray for you"—and I
mean it. But then I forget. Too many things crowd in, and I just
get so busy. Before I know it, the moment has passed, and it's
too late to pray. But I'm so glad Jesus was never like that! He
promised to pray for us—and he never, ever forgets. It's a promise
he's keeping right now.

I'm grateful that, like he did for Simon Peter, he's praying that
my faith may not fail; that I won't lose my faith or give up, whatever might happen; and that my trust in you will remain strong,
despite all the challenges and opposition.

I'm also grateful that he's asking the Father to "keep [me]
safe from the evil one,"[1] who "prowls around like a roaring lion,
looking for someone to devour";[2] and so I need not walk through
this day fearfully.

I'm grateful that Jesus is constantly interceding for me before
your throne, for he intimately knows me and my weaknesses and
can bring all those things to you.

Lord, let this sink in deep and be my reassurance today: Jesus
is praying for me! *Amen.*

---

[1] John 17:15 [2] 1 Peter 5:8

Because Jesus lives forever, his priesthood lasts forever. Therefore he is able, once and forever, to save those who come to God through him. He lives forever to intercede with God on their behalf.

HEBREWS 7:24-25

FOALFOOT
Foalfoot, also known as coltsfoot, is a member of the daisy family; yet its flowers bear a striking resemblance to dandelions.

No Retirement!

Today I am eighty-five years old. I am as strong now as I was when Moses sent me on that journey, and I can still travel and fight as well as I could then. So give me the hill country that the LORD promised me.   JOSHUA 14:10-12

Lord, I'M AMAZED BY CALEB, who spoke these words. He was eighty-five, but he wasn't going to let age stop him. After journeying through the wilderness and playing his part in taking the Promised Land, it was just too much to contemplate stopping before he'd received his own inheritance. He was determined to claim it before he died—and he did.

And I think of Anna, who wasn't planning on retirement either. There she was in the Temple when Jesus' parents came to dedicate him. Now a very old woman, she'd spent her whole life as a prophet preparing for the Messiah's coming. But she was still serving you with all her heart, and she was rewarded by being able to give one last great prophecy over your Son.[1]

Many people these days can't wait for retirement. But thank you that Caleb and Anna remind me that no matter what stage of life I am in, no matter what age I am, no matter what I may or may not have achieved by now, there is no retirement in your Kingdom. The opportunity to do something for you is always there.

So please help me not to write myself off or put myself into early retirement. Help me not to let the passing years discourage me, nor age disqualify me. I simply offer myself to you afresh today for you to use me. *Amen.*

---

[1] Luke 2:36-38

Even in old age they will still produce fruit; they will remain vital and green.

PSALM 92:14

LAVENDER

Provence, France, is famous for lavender fields. California, Australia, and the UK also have them. South Korea hosts the annual Goseong Lavender Festival.

THE GOD
Who Leads

Right behind you a voice will say, "This is the way you should go."

ISAIAH 30:21

Lord, **THERE ARE SO MANY TIMES** when I have to make decisions. Some are about very ordinary, day-to-day things; but others are much more significant. At such times, it's really hard to know the right thing to do. And because I really want to do the right thing, I can even feel paralyzed—overwhelmed by the possibilities or the uncertainties.

But that's when I remember that you really do want to guide me, as your Word constantly shows. Even with an unknown wilderness ahead of them, Moses and the Israelites could sing, "With your unfailing love you lead the people you have redeemed. In your might, you guide them to your sacred home."[1] And as Isaiah said, you are always there, whispering into our ears, telling us which way to take—if only we will listen.

When I'm paralyzed by thoughts of *But what if . . .* , it's good to remember that you, who are outside of time, know all the "what-ifs" of life, for you are the Sovereign God. You know all the conceivable possibilities and options ahead of me—and you have a plan for every single one of them! I may not be able to see around the corner, but you can! And even if I get it wrong, you are still the God who "causes everything to work together for the good of those who love [you]."[2]

So today I claim the promise of your guidance—and I choose to trust you, the God who leads. *Amen.*

---

[1] Exodus 15:13 [2] Romans 8:28

That is what God is like. He is our God forever and ever, and *he will guide us until we die*.

PSALM 48:14

WOOD ANEMONE

Wood anemone is also called windflower. Because the plant spreads very slowly, its presence usually indicates an ancient woodland.

GOD,
Our Redeemer

Praise the LORD, who has now provided a redeemer for your family!

RUTH 4:14

Lord, I CAN HARDLY BEGIN TO IMAGINE how utterly alone Naomi must have felt. She had left Bethlehem with her husband and two sons to avoid famine. But there in Moab, her husband and both of her sons died.

When she heard the famine was over, she decided to return home. Her sons had married Moabite wives, Orpah and Ruth, and she urged them to stay in Moab, knowing there was no way she could provide for them. But although Orpah decided to stay, Ruth was determined to go with Naomi, saying, "Wherever you go, I will go; wherever you live, I will live. Your people will be my people, and your God will be my God. Wherever you die, I will die, and there I will be buried."[1]

I can't imagine the emotions that must have flooded Naomi's heart when she heard those words—words that were the start of your plan of redemption. What amazing "coincidences" then followed! Back in Bethlehem, they *just happened* to meet Boaz, one of Naomi's nearest relatives who had a duty to help them—to be their redeemer. And so he married Ruth, not only providing for her and Naomi but also establishing a family line from which King David—and ultimately Jesus—would come.

---

[1] Ruth 1:16-17

Lord, how you love to redeem situations! And this is still true today . . . and still true for me. No matter what my circumstances might be, no matter how bleak the outlook, you always have a plan to redeem! I thank you for that. *Amen.*

Rise up! Help us!
  Ransom us because of your unfailing love.

PSALM 44:26

LESSER CELANDINE
The yellow-flowered lesser celandine belongs to the Ranunculales order of plants, along with buttercups, poppies, and anemones. It blooms in early spring, then quickly disappears.

GOD CAN TAKE
Your Honesty

> *Because of my imprisonment, most of the believers here*
> *have gained confidence and boldly speak God's message*
> *without fear.* PHILIPPIANS 1:14

Lord, I ALMOST MISSED that word *most* in today's Scripture. *Most* of the believers. So presumably, *not all* of them! *Most* of them gained confidence and became bold because of Paul's example in jail. So some weren't so confident. I suppose they could have been wimps; but probably the truth is they were just ordinary Christians who were being real about their doubts and fears.

If I'm honest, Lord, I'm not always real—either with you or other people. They ask how I am, and I always answer, "Fine!"; but what I really want to say sometimes is, "To be honest, I'm struggling." And sometimes I'm like that with you. I know everyone faces difficulties of one kind or another, at some time or other; why should I pretend I'm any different?

So I'm going to start being more honest with you, Lord. When I'm struggling, I'm going to say so. When I'm doubting, I'm going to acknowledge it. When I'm anxious, I'm going to tell you. And when I'm mad at you, I'm going to let you have it, just as so many in the Bible did. For honesty is the first sign of a good relationship. And when I'm honest with you, that's when you can start to work.

Today I'm being real with you, Lord, so that our relationship can grow, and I can grasp hold of more of your promises and purposes for my life. *Amen.*

I cry out to the LORD; I plead for the LORD's mercy.

*I pour out my complaints before him
and tell him all my troubles.*

PSALM 142:1-2

COW PARSNIP
Cow parsnip grows tall along
the Pacific and Atlantic coasts.
It produces special chemicals
that defend against bugs but
cause rash and blisters
on people.

THE JOY OF

the Lord

This is a sacred day before our Lord. Don't be dejected and sad,
for the joy of the LORD is your strength! NEHEMIAH 8:10

Lord, **WHEREVER JESUS WENT, HE BROUGHT JOY.** And
he took that joy to those written off by the followers of joyless
religion—those they looked down on as "sinners." But as these
"sinners" spent time with Jesus, they rediscovered the joy of life—a
joy that impacted Zacchaeus so much he could say, "I will give
half my wealth to the poor, Lord, and if I have cheated people
on their taxes, I will give them back four times as much!"[1] His joy
must have been deep!

Lord, I'm glad to know you prefer us to be happy rather than
sad! But I recognize that joy isn't restricted to just happy feelings;
joy is about a deep confidence in you, no matter what happens.
That's why Nehemiah could tell your people, "The joy of the Lord
is your strength!" For after all their efforts to rebuild Jerusalem's
walls, they suddenly felt overwhelmed as Ezra read your Word
to them and they realized how much they'd failed you. But what
they needed at that moment, Nehemiah understood, wasn't to
be weighed down with guilt, but to be lifted up through joy—the
joy of knowing you had not abandoned them despite everything.

So today, Lord, no matter what happens, I receive your promises
that through your Holy Spirit I can experience your joy, and that
your joy will be my strength. *Amen.*

---

[1] Luke 19:8

128

The Kingdom of God is not a matter of what we eat or drink, but of living a life of goodness and peace and joy in the Holy Spirit.

ROMANS 14:17

PURPLE DEADNETTLE
In Greek, the scientific name for purple deadnettle means "devouring purple monster." It's a fitting description for the weed's dominant behavior.

GO-GETTERS

for God

> *I, Daniel, learned from reading the word of the LORD,*
> *as revealed to Jeremiah the prophet, that Jerusalem must lie desolate*
> *for seventy years. So I turned to the Lord God and pleaded with*
> *him in prayer and fasting. I also wore rough burlap and*
> *sprinkled myself with ashes.* DANIEL 9:2-3

Lord, **DANIEL WAS A REAL GO-GETTER.** He wasn't one of those people who just sits back in life and thinks that if something is going to happen, it will happen; that whatever will be, will be, and there's nothing we can do about it.

He was confident from reading your Word that your people would return to their land because you had promised it. But he didn't just sit back and think, *It's bound to happen, so I'll just wait for it.* No. He thought, *God has promised this; therefore I will pray it into being.* Your promise was his reason for prayer, not an excuse for inactivity; his reason for activism, not an excuse for fatalism.

And within just a few months, King Darius of Babylon was gone, and King Cyrus of Persia sent the Jews home, just as Jeremiah had said. You promised it; Daniel prayed for it; and then it happened!

Lord, make me that kind of go-getter—one who discovers the promises in your Word and then confidently prays them into being, sure that my prayers are right on target and *will* be answered. May your unfailing promises be both the stimulus and the basis for my prayers! *Amen.*

We are confident that he hears us whenever we ask for anything that pleases him. And since we know he hears us when we make our requests, we also know that he will give us what we ask for.

1 JOHN 5:14-15

SPOTTED CORALROOT
Spotted coralroot spans most of North America. This orchid gets its nutrients mainly from fungi instead of photosynthesis.

No Longer Slaves

Now you are no longer a slave but God's own child. And since you are his child, God has made you his heir. GALATIANS 4:7

Lord, **I CAN'T IMAGINE** what it must have been like to be a slave—just a mere piece of property owned by someone else, to be used as they saw fit and then tossed aside if they wanted, with no hope of freedom. Yet that's what your Word says I was like before I trusted in Jesus. I thought I was free—but I wasn't! I was in slavery to all sorts of things—things that ruled me rather than that I ruled. But thank you that your Son paid the price to set me free.

And Lord, wonderful as that is, it isn't the end of the story. For you didn't just set me free and send me on my way; you made me part of your family, adopting me as your own child! Little wonder John wrote in amazement, "See how very much our Father loves us, for he calls us his children, and that is what we are!"[1]

But it doesn't stop there! For Paul wrote, "Since we are his children, we are his heirs. In fact, together with Christ we are heirs of God's glory."[2] Wow! To think that I'm your heir, with all of heaven's resources now available to me!

So please help me not to live as a slave, saying yes to the old things that used to order me around. Help me to listen to your voice as my new master—the voice of a loving Father speaking to his child; for in responding to that voice, I find both freedom and inheritance. *Amen.*

[1] John 3:1 [2] Romans 8:17

Christ has truly set us free. Now make sure that you stay free.

GALATIANS 5:1

GORSE

Gorse can flourish in less-than-ideal conditions, such as poor, shallow soil. It blooms any time of year, including midwinter.

THE FAMILY

Likeness

God knew his people in advance, and he chose them to become like his Son. ROMANS 8:29

Lord, **IT'S FUNNY HOW** as children grow up, they so often become increasingly like their parents. Certain family characteristics are more obvious: the shape of their noses, how their hair lies, the way they walk or stand or say things. The family likeness begins to show.

And that's what you want for your people too—to show the family likeness, just like Jesus did. He spoke with your kindness, acted with your compassion, healed with your tenderness, gave with your generosity, forgave with your grace . . . In fact, he resembled you so much that he could say to his disciples, "Anyone who has seen me has seen the Father!"[1]

But you don't want the family likeness to stop with him; you want us—me!—to reflect the family likeness too. I know I could never reflect everything that you are, Father; but I can reflect something of it, and that's what I want to do.

I'm grateful that you haven't left me alone in this. You've sent your Holy Spirit to fill me and live within me, working on me from the inside out, so that as I let him do his work, I can be increasingly transformed into your likeness.

So today, Lord, I ask you to let more and more of the family likeness be seen in me. *Amen.*

---

[1] John 14:9

All of us who have had that veil removed can see and

reflect the glory of the Lord.

And the Lord—who is the Spirit—makes us more and more
like him as we are changed into his glorious image.

2 CORINTHIANS 3:18

COMMON TOADFLAX
Common toadflax thrives on
waste ground and roadsides.
Often mistaken for snapdragon, its
butter-yellow and orange blooms
contribute to its other name,
"butter and eggs."

GOD'S GOODNESS
and Ours

You are good and do only good. PSALM 119:68

Lord, WE CHRISTIANS OFTEN GET DISMISSED as "do-gooders." But help me not to be ashamed of that label, for I know your heart for us is always that we should do good. Not because doing good is how we get to know you or win your favor or work our way to heaven—that comes through trusting in your Son, Jesus, alone. No, you want us to do good quite simply because you yourself *are* good; and because you *are* good, all that you *do* is good; and because you are good and do good, all your promises can be trusted to bring about good too.

That's why Joshua, toward the end of his life, could tell your people, "Deep in your hearts you know that every promise of the LORD your God has come true. Not a single one has failed!"[1] He understood that your faithful fulfilling of all the promises you had made was just another expression of your goodness.

And it's because you have been so good to us, just as you promised, that you call on us as your children to reflect your goodness by sharing it with others—and not just with friends, but even with those who are enemies. For goodness in our lives can begin to open people up to you, our good God, and to seeing what you are really like.

So Lord, help me not to be afraid of being known as a "do-gooder." Rather, help me to reflect the family likeness by enjoying more of your promised goodness myself and then passing it on.

Amen.

---

[1] Joshua 23:14

Do what is right and good

in the LORD's sight, so all will go well with you.

DEUTERONOMY 6:18

HAZEL

Male and female hazel flowers grow on the same shrub. Females are fertilized when the wind blows pollen from the male clusters, producing tasty hazelnuts.

WHEN
Trouble Comes

**The LORD is good, a strong refuge when trouble comes.
He is close to those who trust in him.** NAHUM 1:7

Lord, **TROUBLES SEEM TO HAVE A WAY** of coming all at once. So often, life has been going wonderfully when suddenly someone gets sick; problems arise at work; the children are struggling in school; the car breaks down; I suffer a major disappointment; an unexpected bill arrives. And at times like that, Lord, it's really good to know who I can turn to.

Your servant Nahum certainly lived in troubled times. Assyria, who had already conquered Samaria some years earlier, was now eyeing Judah. But in the midst of this trouble, Nahum declared in faith that Assyria would experience your judgment for all its cruelty—and it did soon afterward. But in the meantime, Nahum—whose very name means "comfort"—reassured your people that you were still good and still cared, and that you were a strong refuge for all who trust you.

Lord, thank you that you are still that strong refuge today. Thank you that whenever I'm facing trouble, you don't want me to pretend everything is okay, nor to run around like a crazy person, panicking and trying to fix things. Rather, you invite me to honestly bring the trouble to you and to make you my refuge until it is past.

So when trouble comes next, may I not just say, "Here comes trouble!" but may I also say, "Here comes the Lord, too!" *Amen.*

He will conceal me there when troubles come; he will hide me in his sanctuary.

He will place me out of reach on a high rock.

PSALM 27:5

LARCH FLOWER

Larch trees are conifers whose short, green needles turn yellow and fall off in autumn. Their pink cone-like flowers eventually harden into brown pine cones.

THE CALL TO
Kindness

*Get rid of all bitterness, rage, anger, harsh words, and slander, as
well as all types of evil behavior. Instead, be kind to each other,
tenderhearted, forgiving one another, just as God through Christ
has forgiven you.*   EPHESIANS 4:31-32

Lord, THERE OFTEN ISN'T A LOT OF KINDNESS in the world
today. People are so self-focused, so busy with their own lives
that they rarely stop to think of others. And when kindness is
demonstrated in some way, it really hits people as something
unusual. Yet kindness should be completely normal.

Again and again you call us in your Word to be kind. Why?
Because you yourself are kind! Your Son, Jesus, is the very incarnation of kindness, having spent his whole earthly life being kind
to others—healing the sick, giving hope to the hopeless, providing for the needy, accepting the rejected, forgiving those who
sinned. And he wasn't just kind; he was kind to those who didn't
deserve it. For even as wicked men were nailing him to the cross,
he was still being kind, offering forgiveness to one of those crucified with him.[1] How incredibly kind! But this is what you are like,
Lord—always offering your kindness freely to all, even to those
who don't deserve it.

Lord, it is only as we understand how very kind you are to us
that we will in turn pass on that kindness to others. So please
grow more of this fruit of the Spirit in me as I seek to share your
kindness with all those I come into contact with today. *Amen.*

---

[1] Luke 23:32-43

Love is patient and kind.

Love is not jealous or boastful or proud or rude. It does not demand its own way. It is not irritable, and it keeps no record of being wronged.

1 CORINTHIANS 13:4-5

PURPLE CORNFLOWER
Purple cornflower looks like a purple variety of the blue cornflower. Its name can be easily confused with the purple *coneflower*, or echinacea.

Changes Things

Speak, LORD, your servant is listening. 1 SAMUEL 3:9

Lord, **LISTENING IS A REMARKABLE GIFT**, and all too few of us use it. Yet your Word shows how listening can really change things. That's certainly something Samuel discovered.

As a "miracle baby," he'd been dedicated to your service even before his conception. Entrusted to Eli at the Tabernacle in Shiloh, he grew in favor with you and others, but he still didn't know you, not yet having had a personal encounter with you. But all that was about to change—and all because he listened.

It happened when messages from you "were very rare, and visions were quite uncommon."[1] But Samuel suddenly found himself hearing your voice—though at first he didn't recognize it. He just thought Eli was calling him. But after Samuel awakened Eli the third time, Eli realized it must have been you who were speaking. And so Eli told Samuel to do something very simple, yet incredibly important: listen.

And through that listening, Samuel began a long and distinguished career as the prophet who steered Israel out of its dark days and prepared the way for Israel's first king—a wonderfully successful ministry, which all began with *listening*. Had he not listened, who knows how history may have unfolded?

---

[1] 1 Samuel 3:1

Lord, I believe you still want to speak today, so please help me to listen more and more. And then help me to be obedient to what you say so that like Samuel, you can use me, too, to be a blessing to those around me. *Amen.*

Come and listen to what the LORD your God says.

JOSHUA 3:9

SPURGE LAUREL

Birds love spurge laurel, although it's dangerous to humans and pets. Native to Europe and the Mediterranean, it grows in versatile environments but favors shade.

My Daddy!

Because we are his children, God has sent the Spirit of his Son into our hearts, prompting us to call out, "Abba, Father." GALATIANS 4:6

Lord, I LOVE TO SEE a young child rushing into their father's presence, no matter who might be around, and shouting, "Daddy!" as they throw themselves into his arms. But what I love even more is how Jesus told us that we can relate to you in exactly the same way!

Calling you "Father" was a normal part of Jesus' life, even though no one else did. But not only did he call you "Father"—he also called you "Abba"—an Aramaic word that children used, meaning "daddy." And what I find amazing is how Jesus used this most intimate and trusting of words at the very moment when he could have had cause for doubting you—in the garden of Gethsemane. For it is there, in the midst of his agonies, that we find him praying, "Abba, Father."[1] Such trust in your fatherly care, even when things didn't look good!

But Lord, what is even more amazing is that Jesus didn't keep this word *Abba* to himself; he extended the privilege to us—to me!—through the Holy Spirit, who "joins with our spirit to affirm that we are God's children."[2] You are now our Abba, my Abba! Not a cold, formal father but a Father who loves me and is intimate with me; a Father into whose arms I can throw myself and shout, "Daddy!"

So today I thank you that you are *fatherly* in everything you do and in your intimate knowledge of me and care for me. *Amen.*

---

[1] Mark 14:36 [2] Romans 8:16

144

You received God's Spirit when he adopted you as his own children. Now we call him, "*Abba, Father.*"

ROMANS 8:15

GREATER CELANDINE
Greater celandine is a potent herb that is part of the poppy family. It has been used medicinally for centuries in many cultures.

THE BLESSING OF

True Friends

Two people are better off than one, for they can help each other succeed. If one person falls, the other can reach out and help. But someone who falls alone is in real trouble.

ECCLESIASTES 4:9-10

Lord, **WHAT A BLESSING IT IS** to have friends who love us, come what may; who stand by us through thick and thin; who are there for us when we need them; who don't try to "fix" us, but simply listen. The Bible has so many examples of these kinds of friends: Moses with Joshua; Ruth with Naomi; David with Jonathan; Jesus with Mary, Martha, and Lazarus; Paul with Timothy. Such rich examples of true, loyal friendship.

But Lord, I'm also mindful that a true friend isn't afraid to challenge us and tell us the truth when we need it; to confront us, not in anger but in love—just like Jethro did with Moses,[1] and Nathan did with David,[2] and Paul did with Peter;[3] for "wounds from a sincere friend are better than many kisses from an enemy."[4]

It always feels better to be praised than to be challenged, to be affirmed than confronted. But help me to build such deep friendships that when my friends confront me, I know it is *because* they love me and want your best for me.

So today, I thank you for my friends and ask you to bless them.

---

[1] Exodus 18:13-27 [2] 2 Samuel 12:1-14 [3] Galatians 2:11-14 [4] Proverbs 27:6

I also ask you to deepen my friendships with them so that we can love and confront one another, and so help each other to keep pressing on in our Christian journeys. *Amen.*

There are "friends" who destroy each other, but

a real friend sticks closer than a brother.

PROVERBS 18:24

HYSSOP
In Bible times, hyssop was used in purification ceremonies. Its flowers bloom from summer to fall, attracting insects that would otherwise harm vital food crops.

the Whispers

After the wind there was an earthquake, but the LORD was not in the earthquake. And after the earthquake there was a fire, but the LORD was not in the fire. And after the fire there was the sound of a gentle whisper. 1 KINGS 19:11-12

Lord, LIFE CAN BE SO FULL OF ACTIVITY, so full of noise. That's how it was for Elijah when he experienced the exciting demonstrations of your power in his contest with Baal's prophets on Mount Carmel. After that, he was completely exhausted—so exhausted that when Queen Jezebel threatened him, he ran. What he needed right then was to experience not your power, but your presence.

As Elijah stood on Mount Sinai, where he had fled, there was a great wind, followed by an earthquake and a fire—traditional ways in which you had manifested your power and through which he probably expected to meet you again. But to his surprise, you weren't in any of them. But then you crept up on him, unexpectedly, in "the sound of a gentle whisper." And that's when you spoke to him—in the stillness.

Lord, your Word often calls us to be still before you—not because stillness is more holy than noise, but because being still gives us the opportunity to experience what we might otherwise miss—to simply remember again who you are, and to see everything in light of that.

I find being still a challenge, Lord. So please help me learn to stop—and to be ready to wait for your whispers. *Amen.*

Those who trust in the LORD will find new strength.
They will soar high on wings like eagles.
They will run and not grow weary.
They will walk and not faint.

ISAIAH 40:31

BIRD CHERRY TREE
Strongly scented white flowers from the bird cherry tree bud in early spring. After pollination from insects, they produce dark red, bitter cherries.

Pressing On

Forgetting the past and looking forward to what lies ahead, I press on to reach the end of the race and receive the heavenly prize for which God, through Christ Jesus, is calling us. PHILIPPIANS 3:13-14

Lord, **THERE ARE TIMES** when I find it hard to keep going—especially when I've let you down. I sometimes even feel like I'm going backward in my Christian life rather than forward. There I am, trying to be like Jesus, trying to love and follow him, when suddenly I stumble. And what's worse is that sometimes I do it deliberately.

I know this is because there's a battle going on within me. Sin, forgiven though it is, is still at work. There's a war between the surviving desires of my old sinful nature and the growing desires of the new nature that Christ has given me. Like Paul, sometimes I feel that "I don't really understand myself, for I want to do what is right, but I don't do it. Instead, I do what I hate."[1]

But Lord, I don't want to give in to this! I don't want to accept that it's just how things are and that I'll have to live with it until I get to heaven. I want to remember Paul's encouragement not to get bogged down in what has been, but to keep pressing on toward the prize that Jesus has won for me.

So today, Lord, help me to keep pressing on with you. *Amen.*

---

[1] Romans 7:15

Since we are surrounded by such a huge crowd of witnesses to the life of faith, let us strip off every weight that slows us down, especially the sin that so easily trips us up. And let us run with endurance the race God has set before us.

HEBREWS 12:1

GOLDENROD

A member of the sunflower family, goldenrod is famous for its many nutritional benefits. Its nectar attracts a wide variety of insects—especially bees.

IMAGE CREDITS